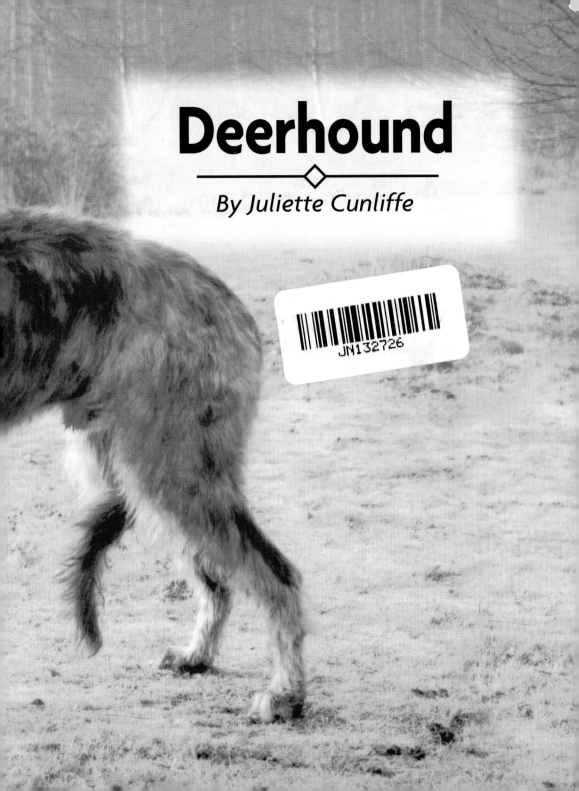

# Deerhound

◇

## By Juliette Cunliffe

# CONTENTS

Travel through antiquity to discover the true origins of this age-old sighthound from Scotland. From early written references to the Deerhound to historical accounts of the breed by early promoters of this breed, the Deerhound's is a fascinating story. Trace the rise of this fashionable rough-haired greyhound at the side of Queen Victoria, its presence at the shows in England, the struggles of early breeders and its exportation to American shores and beyond.

Discover whether the Deerhound is the right dog for you. Learn about the breed's personality, its sizeable requirements, amicability with other pets and children, and much more. The potential owner is also made aware of the various hereditary problems known in the breed that concern breeders today.

Learn the requirements of a well-bred Deerhound by studying the description of the breed as set forth in The Kennel Club's breed standard. Both show dogs and pets must possess key characteristics as outlined in the breed standard.

Be advised about choosing a reputable breeder and selecting a healthy, typical puppy. Understand the responsibilities of ownership, including home preparation, acclimatisation, the vet and prevention of common puppy problems.

Enter into a sensible discussion of dietary and feeding considerations, exercise, grooming, travelling and identification of your dog. This chapter discusses Deerhound care for all stages of development.

PUBLISHED IN THE UNITED KINGDOM BY:

**INTERPET**
PUBLISHING
Vincent Lane, Dorking, Surrey RH4 3YX England

ISBN 1-903098-82-3

PHOTOGRAPHS BY CAROL ANN JOHNSON
with additional photos by Norvia Behling, TJ Calhoun, Carolina Biological Supply, Doskocil, Isabelle Francais, James Hayden-Yoav, James R Hayden, RBP, Bill Jonas, Dwight R Kuhn, Dr Dennis Kunkel, Mikki Pet Products, Phototake, Jean Claude Revy, Dr Andrew Spielman, Steve Surfman and Alice van Kempen.

The publisher wishes to thank Jennifer Cooper, Juliette Cunliffe, Carol Ann Johnson, Glenis & Mick Peach and the rest of the owners of the dogs featured in this book.

Illustrations by Patricia Peters

# History of the
# DEERHOUND

The Deerhound of Scotland hunts primarily by sight and owes its origin to the Greyhound of England. Through the centuries there have been various rough-coated greyhounds, and the Deerhound has sometimes been confused with the Irish Wolfhound. However, there is a substantial difference between these two breeds, with the Wolfhound possessing a much heavier frame, and the Deerhound carrying a head that is closer to that of the Greyhound.

The Deerhound is a breed of great antiquity. It is likely that the breed was kept in Scotland in the middle of the 16th century, and there are several references to dogs of Deerhound type in subsequent centuries. In 1637 Aldrovandus showed a dog clearly resembling the breed, but he called it a 'White Hairy Greyhound.' He did not mention that the dog was from Scotland, even though he had referred to other dogs from that area. However, a drawing by Abraham Hondius, dated 1682, very clearly depicts a Deerhound.

Written evidence of the breed

'The Deer Stalkers' by Landseer, engraved by Finden, shows deer hunters with their Deerhounds in Scotland during the 1800s.

The Deerhound is a very old breed, with evidence of Deerhound-type dogs dating back to the 16th century.

first appeared in 1769 when Pennant visited Gordon Castle. He describes a large dog, covered with long hair and used by the Scottish chiefs in stag chases. This he called 'the true Highland Greyhound' and commented that the breed had by then become very scarce.

We learn from Ralph Beilby's *A General History of Quadrupeds* (1790) that what he called the 'Scottish Highland Greyhound or Wolfdog' was formerly used by Scottish chieftains in their grand hunting parties. We can see that this splendid breed, 'its eyes half hid in hair,' was certainly on the decline, for Beilby mentioned one that had been seen some years previously. Its body was strong, muscular and covered with harsh, wiry, reddish hair, mixed with white. According to the *Encyclopaedia Britannica*, only a year later the 'Highland Grehound' had become very scarce,

> **DID YOU KNOW?**
> Despite there having been 60 deer forests in Britain, shortly before the First World War only six remained in which Deerhounds were kept for sporting purposes. In the words of Robert Leighton, '...the inventions of the modern gunsmith have robbed one of the grandest of hunting dogs of his glory, relegating him to the life of a pedestrian pet....'

but mention is made of this breed's being as fierce as the Bloodhound and with as 'sagacious nostrils.'

## SIR WALTER SCOTT'S MAIDA

For many people, the first Deerhound that springs immediately to mind is Sir Walter Scott's Maida. In fact, Maida had a Deerhound dam and a Pyrenean sire, the latter giving some white to Maida's coat, but in most respects he looked like a

**MISS NORAH HARTLEY**

Until a few years ago, we were fortunate enough still to have in our midst Miss Norah Hartley of the Rotherwood Deerhounds. This remarkable lady not only kept accurate records of her own dogs but also housed a veritable wealth of information about the breed in her magnificent home.

Deerhound. Although Maida looked much like his dam, his sire gave him strength and power. We can learn a great deal about Maida from Washington Irving, who described this magnificent dog as 'a giant in iron grey.'

Maida had a grave demeanour, and most of the time acted with decorum and dignity. When the younger dogs leapt on his neck and worried his ears, he would sometimes rebuke them, but when alone with the dogs he would play the boy as much as any of them. However, Irving felt Maida was ashamed to do so when in company and commented that he seemed to say, 'Ha! Done with your nonsense, youngsters. What will the laird and that other

A recent gift to the Maxwell-Scotts is this statue of Sir Walter Scott's Deerhound Maida.

SIR WALTER SCOTTS GREAT HOUND. MAIDA

Two Deerhounds flank the statue of Maida, under which lie his remains. Maida still guards the door of Abbotsford, where Sir Walter lived.

A scene at Abbotsford, showing Sir Walter Scott's dogs, Maida and Torrum. From a painting by Sir Edwin Landseer, RA.

Deerhound lovers and their dogs, visiting the home of Sir Walter Scott.

In the dining room, the room in which Sir Walter Scott died overlooking his beloved River Tweed, is this small replica of Edinburgh's monument to Sir Walter, with Maida at his feet.

gentleman think of me if I give way to such foolery?'

How fortunate we are today that a member of this magnificent breed was owned by a great poet like Sir Walter Scott, who used his considerable talents to render the Deerhound so memorably: 'The most perfect creature of Heaven.' Scott likened Maida's bark to the great guns of Constantinople: '...it takes so long to get it ready, that the smaller guns can fire off a dozen times first; but when it goes off, it plays the very devil.'

Maida died peacefully in 1822, and by early in the 20th century it was believed that many of the best Deerhounds of their day were descended from him. However, when Maida died, there was something of a rumpus, for the inscription on his epitaph carried an error in Latin. This was copied in the press and vexed Scott, a man to whom the written word was so sacred. Maida was buried at the door of Abbotsford, where his remains still lie and the inscription, translated, reads:

> *Beneath the sculptured form which late you wore, Sleep soundly, Maida, at your master's door.*

Yet Maida lives on in many ways, for there is no doubt that in Scott's *Woodstock Bevis* was actually the author's favourite hound, Maida.

**ACCORDING TO SCROPE**

*The Art of Deerstalking*, written by William Scrope and published in 1838, confirms how numerically weak the breed was as that time. Scrope claimed to have a perfect knowledge of every specimen of the breed in Scotland, which he thought numbered only a dozen pure Deerhounds. He was at pains to point out the differences between the Irish Wolfhound and the Scottish Deerhound, but thought that some degeneracy had taken place. This was due in part to the reduced number, but also because of neglect in crossing, selection and feeding. He believed that in earlier days Deerhounds had

Patricia Maxwell-Scott (left) greets Deerhounds and their owners at the entrance gate to Abbotsford.

measured some 76 cms (30 inches) in height and 86 cms (34 inches) in girth, and weighed 47 kgs (103.5 lbs).

Despite his belief that the breed had degenerated, Scrope still believed that no other member of the canine race had such a combination of qualities: speed, strength, size, endurance, courage, perseverance, sagacity, docility, elegance and dignity. What more can one say about the breed? Scrope has said it all!

## CROSSES WITH THE DEERHOUND

Various attempts were made to improve the Deerhound by crossing it with other breeds but, in Scrope's opinion, all had utterly failed. Crossing with the Bulldog had added courage, but had resulted in loss of speed, strength and weight. Crossing with the Bloodhound increased the power of smell, but speed and size were diminished. When the Pyrenean Wolfdog was used for the purpose of crossing, some increase in weight was produced but both speed and courage were lost.

## SOME OF THE EARLY DOGS

Breed enthusiasts today are fortunate indeed that through the centuries Deerhound lovers have kept accurate records of their hounds. Scrope considered that four of the finest specimens of the breed at that time belonged to

## KANGAROO DOGS

In Australia, Deerhound blood has been infused with that of the Greyhound to create Kangaroo Dogs, also sometimes known as Staghounds. Kangaroo Dogs have for decades been fast enough to catch game for their owners, and have also been strong enough to kill dingoes that have attacked the flocks. Kangaroo Dogs have been exhibited at Australia's Royal Agricultural Shows.

Typical Irish Wolfhound, another sighthound to which the Deerhound has frequently been compared.

Captain McNeill of Colonsay. These were the now infamous males, Buskar and Bran, and two bitches, Runa and Cavak. Two were pale yellow in colour, the others a sandy red. Although quality and length of their hair varied, all had black tips to their ears, and their eyes and muzzles were black. Important too was that each of them was a uniform colour, something Scrope considered an indication of purity.

Buskar was measured and weighed in 1836, his height recorded as 71 cms (28 inches) and his weight in running

condition as 38.5 kgs (85 lbs) . Scrope noted a remarkable difference in size between dogs and bitches, a difference he thought more remarkable than in any

## A DEERHOUND OF MANY NAMES

The Deerhound has acquired many names through its history. In the USA, it is called the Scottish Deerhound. Other names that are no longer used include the Scotch Greyhound, Rough Greyhound, Irish Wolf Dog and Highland Deerhound.

other species of canine.

Another valuable comparison made by Scrope was the difference in measurements between a Deerhound and a fully-grown stag. No wonder, he said, that few dogs, if any, were capable of bringing down a stag single-handed. A stag's height at the shoulder was almost 122 cms (48 inches) and the extreme height from the top of the antlers to the ground was 235 cms (7 ft 10 ins). As he fell, this particular stag weighed 145 kgs (310 lbs).

In the Highlands, dark-grey-coloured coats had been more prevalent than the yellowish or reddish colours, but grey coats were generally softer and more woolly than the latter.

### THE SCOTTISH GREYHOUND

Like Scrope, John Meyrick was a 19th-century author from whom we learn much about the Deerhound. In 1861 he wrote about Queen Victoria's Deerhound, commenting that he knew of no other pure-bred Deerhound in the country. In his opinion, some were called Deerhounds but they were in fact Scottish Greyhounds, although some undoubtedly had some true Deerhound blood. Others were crossed with the Bloodhound or some other breed.

**The head of a Deerhound as sketched in the early 1800s.**

## BRAIN AND BRAWN

Since dogs have been inbred for centuries, their physical and mental characteristics are constantly being changed to suit man's desires for hunting, retrieving, scenting, guarding and warming their masters' laps. During the past 150 years, dogs have been judged according to physical characteristics as well as functional abilities. Few breeds can boast a genuine balance between physique, working ability and temperament.

There continue to be differences of opinion as to whether the Scottish Greyhound and the Deerhound were, in fact, one and the same, but Meyrick informed his readers that although the former resembled the Deerhound both in colour and in shape, it was considerably smaller. Most Scottish Greyhounds were below 66 cms (26 inches) in height.

### A FASHIONABLE HOUND

Queen Victoria was a great lady whose opinions influenced the entire world, including the world of pure-dogs. Several breeds owe something of their revival to the fact that Her Majesty owned the breed, thereby bringing it to public attention.

Deerhounds were kept in Queen Victoria's kennels both at Windsor and at Sandringham, where they were cared for by Mr Cole. Indeed, this gentleman became so connected with Her Majesty's hounds that some dogs became known as the 'Mr Cole breed.' When the Queen and Prince Albert were in residence at Balmoral, they had with them Solomon, Hector and Bran. Bran became wonderfully famous, for he was depicted in Landseer's painting *High Life*. He was reputed to be an exceptionally fine dog, standing over 76 cms (30 inches) at shoulder. Another particularly famous Deerhound belonging to the Queen was

Today's Deerhound, a pet and estate guard, is prized for his courage and beauty in many countries.

Keildar, who was used for hunting deer in Windsor Park.

## DEERHOUNDS AT EARLY SHOWS

At the first Manchester Dog Show, held at Bellvue Zoological Gardens in 1861, Deerhounds were one of only a few breeds that were separately classified, albeit with only one class. By 1863, Deerhounds had mustered up a 'fair entry' and that same year at the Birmingham Show, the Duke of Beaufort took along some Deerhounds, among other breeds, and came away with several prizes.

In 1869 Queen Victoria exhibited four of her Deerhounds at Islington in London, and indeed the breed continued to be scheduled with some consistency throughout the next decade.

## THE 19TH CENTURY DRAWS TO ITS CLOSE

By the end of the 19th century, the Deerhound was somewhat smaller in size with only a few larger dogs to be found. One of these was Lord Bredalbane's King

The champion of champions, St. Ronan's Rhyme, born 23 February 1903. It was written that she was 'probably the most perfect dog of any breed at present living.'

The Misses Loughrey's Idric of Ross (left) and Ch Phorp of the Foothills at Crufts in 1934. 'Phorp' won first prize and was the Best Deerhound in the show.

of the Forest, who stood 84 cms (33 inches).

Upon his return from India, Captain Graham had set up his own kennel of Deerhounds, where he intended, as he put it, to 'rebuild' the Irish Wolfhound. In February 1870, he purchased from Mr Cole's widow the Deerhound Keildar, who had been renowned for hunting deer at Windsor and was described as one of the most elegant and aristocratic-looking Deerhounds ever seen. This was an interesting introduction to his kennel, for this dog had as a grandsire a black Russian Wolfhound. Also in the pedigree was Tank, a dog bought by Mr Cole from Tankerville Castle in 1858.

Size was a constant topic of conversation, and in 1872 an informative list of heights was published. Most of the males measured 71 cms (28 inches), the smallest just half an inch less and the largest 77 cms (30.5 inches). The highest proportion for bitches measured 66 cms (26 inches); none was smaller, but one was 74 cms (29 inches).

Undoubtedly, in the mid-19th century, Deerhounds were varied indeed. Some had good hard coats, others had woolly ones, almost resembling the coat of a sheep. Indeed, even today, faulty coat textures come through from time to time, the worst of them known as 'woollies.' There were certainly some dogs that were full

By the 1880s Captain Graham had drawn up a list of the most notable Deerhounds of the previous hundred years. Of these, Torrum seems to have been the most notable stud dog, described as a 'grand specimen of his race, strong framed, with plenty of hair of a blue brindle colour.'

E Watson Bell's book, published in 1892, expressed the author's opinion that the judges of his day had 'fads.' Bell made some interesting comments about the eye of the Deerhound, which, he said, should resemble the 'eye of the terrier as nearly as possible.' He had been given this description of the eye by an experienced old breeder, but such an eye had almost been lost due

**Revis of Rotherwood was a fine example of Miss Norah Hartley's quality Deerhound breeding.**

of quality, but others were very coarse, and some poor specimens of the breed gained their championship titles, a happening that rarely occurs in Britain today.

**Ernest G Chapman drew this head study to show prominent features of the Deerhound: harsh, strong coat, gentleness of eye, small ear and the fine long lines of the muzzle.**

to the crosses made with the Bulldog and Bloodhound. The small eye, he considered, was of great use to the breed, for it enabled the dog to see a greater distance than did a round one.

By then the breed was labouring under a mixture of strains; breeders were so confused that they were producing many different kinds of Deerhounds. Although the black smooth-eared dog had a most striking appearance, this somewhat detracted from the shaggy, rough, Highland tyke-like look that was characteristic of the breed.

## DEERHOUND COLOUR

As the dog world moved into the 20th century, the colour favoured by breeders for Deerhounds on the show bench was dark blue or grey brindle, though in earlier years the light fawn colour had been more desirable. The reason that the lighter Deerhounds had been preferred was said to have been because they could more easily be seen on the hillside.

Many colours were bred just before the century turned,

It was written that 'there is no more docile breed than the Deerhound,' as shown by this young Deerhound and his young mistress.

Some of Miss Hartley's Deerhounds. Like all breeds in the Greyhound family, Deerhounds carry their tails in the characteristic manner.

The Royal Art Collection features the Landseer painting entitled 'The Deer Drive.' In this section of the painting, note the hunters holding their Deerhounds.

including blue brindle, fawn brindle, red brindle, red, fawn, sandy and 'almost black and white.' White, though, was not considered an acceptable colour within the breed, for it denoted crossbreeding. White markings were considered a sign of impure blood, although a little white on toes and chest was 'passable.'

### THE DEERHOUND CLUB

In 1892 the Deerhound Club was formed. Even today in Britain, this is the only club for this breed recognised by The Kennel Club. Thanks to the Deerhound Club, the crosses came to a halt, and a standard of breed points was drawn up, which was

### DID YOU KNOW?

In the US, since 1935 the points of the Deerhound have been arranged in order of importance. They read: Typical, Movements, As tall as possible consistent with quality, Head, Body, Forelegs, Thighs, Loins, Coat, Feet, Ears, Eyes, Neck, Shoulders, Chest, Tail, Teeth and, finally, Nails.

endorsed at a meeting held in Shrewsbury in June 1901. Whether or not it was right to have curtailed crosses was a matter for debate, for the breed by then had not yet fully recovered. However, the breed just about managed to hold its own in the years that followed.

This well-known head portrait was popular with Deerhound lovers in the 1920s.

Since then, the Deerhound has remained in the hands of some highly dedicated breeders, and some notable dogs have achieved very high honours in the show ring. It is still not particularly numerically strong, but this is a very special breed and genuine enthusiasts are happy to keep it that way.

**THE DEERHOUND IN THE USA**
The Scottish Deerhound, as it is still known in America, was first registered by the American Kennel Club (AKC) in 1886. The

The Misses Loughrey's Magnetic of Ross was the winner of the Challenge Certificate at the Birmingham show in 1933.

breed standard is basically the same as that of The Kennel Club, with a few minor variations. A

A modern, high-quality British-bred Deerhound.

## CLUB TO THE RESCUE!

The Deerhound Club has always helped its members through difficult times. During the Second World War, several Deerhounds were 'evacuated' to breed enthusiasts living in less dangerous rural areas. About 16 breeders managed to keep stock through the war years, and by the end of 1944 there was still an enthusiastic band ready to carry on.

white blaze on the forehead or a white collar are reasons for disqualification, whereas in Britain they are only considered 'unacceptable.'

Deerhounds are not used on antlered game in the US, since it is illegal to hunt deer or other antlered game with dogs.

The late Miss Anastasia Noble, a well-known breeder whose Ardkinglas kennels in Britain produced many fine representatives of the breed.

However, the breed has been effective on other game, such as coyotes, wolves and rabbit.

The national parent club is the Scottish Deerhound Club of America, whose purpose is to safeguard the breed and its best interest in the US. It publishes the official newsletter, *The Claymore*, six times per year. It contains information about the breed in the US as well as Canada, Europe and beyond, as well helpful information about health and husbandry, litter announcements and future events, such as National and Regional specialities, breed seminars and lure coursing.

In 1994 the AKC held its inaugural National Lure Coursing Championship at Mt. Holly in New Jersey. This was won by a 14-month-old Scottish Deerhound.

While the breed has a loyal following in the US, it remains among the lesser known breeds, ranking in the bottom sixth of breed registration.

## DID YOU KNOW?

The story of Beth Gelert surely ranks among one of the most loved canine poems ever written. Deerhound enthusiasts say that Beth Gelert was a Deerhound, but Irish Wolfhound followers lay claim to him, too! Sadly, the story is only fable. In fact, there are strong similarities between this story and folklore of other European countries as well as India.

The Deerhound is fortunate to have a devoted following of breeders and enthusiasts working for the continued best interests and betterment of the breed.

The author having a chat with her Deerhound. Along with being friendly and docile, the Deerhound also seems to be a great listener!

## Characteristics of the

# DEERHOUND

There is something very special about the Deerhound that attracts genuine devotees. This is a breed that immediately conjures up images of the life it used to lead in baronial halls, and outstalking deer in the Scottish Highlands. Times have changed, but in essence the Deerhound has not. This is truly a grand animal, a dog that carries himself with quiet dignity.

Those of us who adore the breed seem to be besotted by them, and understandably so. However, this is most certainly not a breed for everyone. The Deerhound is of great size, and though it can sometimes take up surprisingly little space when curled up in a ball, it can look very different when sprawled across your sofa, when sleeping in front of the hearth or when roaming at table-height around the kitchen or dining room!

A Deerhound requires space, exercise and a certain amount of strength. Although for years many lady Deerhound owners, some of them elderly, have made a remark-able sight walking with several well-behaved Deerhounds, it should always be remembered that these ladies have in many cases almost grown up with their hounds. They know how to handle them and how to gain and keep their respect. Such a relationship is not achieved overnight!

Another thing to consider is that the Deerhound, being a large dog, requires much more food than one of the smaller breeds. It can accelerate quickly and run fast, so it also needs a suitable garden or paddock with a secure high boundary. Moreover, owners should bear in mind that although they may love large dogs, not everyone does. Although unlikely to intend any harm, an enormous unrestrained Deerhound approaching a child or adult can be frightening, and there is always the possibility that someone frail could be bowled over inadver-tently!

## PERSONALITY
Keen in the field and gentle in the home, the Deerhound should have a friendly temperament. It should be docile and good-tempered. These aspects of its personality

are very important features of the breed, for a Deerhound is a large, powerful animal; if temperament were not easy, the breed would be very difficult to handle. Unfortunately, there can be the very occasional exception, but in general Deerhounds live up to their breed standard requirements regarding temperament. They should never be suspicious, aggressive nor nervous.

Any indication of ill temper should be dealt with at the very first sign. This must be corrected immediately and firmly, so that the Deerhound always knows who is in charge. This is a breed that is obedient, and is therefore easy to train because of its will to please. The late Miss Norah Hartley of the Rotherwood hounds described the Deerhound as 'obedient and gentle, trusting and unsuspicious.' She thought, too, that the breed was always ready to provide

*Despite the Deerhound's size, Jemma doesn't seem to think she takes up a lot of space. The author's Deerhound takes her ease in a favourite chair.*

> ## A REMEDY FOR WAX
> When candle wax has dripped somewhere it shouldn't have, it can be removed by rubbing with a wad of Deerhound hair. The wax clings to the hound's hair, and this solution to the problem apparently does not damage even a fine antique finish.

companionship to those who valued those qualities. How right she was! A Deerhound undoubtedly seems to understand the mood of his owner, rejoicing in the gaiety of a happy mood, and yet noticing the sobriety of less joyful times and responding accordingly.

### SIZE
Although not so heavy as some breeds of comparable height, the Deerhound is very large and this should never be overlooked. For dogs, the minimum height at withers should be 76 cms (30 ins); bitches should be at least 71 cms (28 ins). Males are generally more substantially built than bitches and should weigh about 45.5 kgs (100 lbs), while the bitches when fully-grown are about 36.5 kgs (80 lbs).

There are no two ways about it: however good the temperament, a Deerhound is a powerful dog, strong enough and with sufficient endurance to pull down a stag. When considering taking on a Deerhound, it is essential always to bear this in mind and to be certain that your personal and family situation, as well as your home environment, are suitable for a dog of this strength and size.

## DEERHOUNDS AND OTHER PETS

Many Deerhound owners are devoted only to the breed and choose not to keep any other type of dog. However, there are other owners who keep them alongside other breeds and, managed sensibly, this need not present a problem. In my own experience, my Deerhound enjoyed the company of other dogs, both large and small. Having said that, when a Deerhound is in the company of small breeds, I am always aware of the damage that could be done if an awkward situation were allowed to get out of hand. I am certainly conscious of the occasional elderly or infirmed Lhasa Apso, who would be all too ready to stand her ground when things did not quite go her way. In such circumstances I am cautious which dogs I leave alone together, and which I do not.

On the other hand, I have had many a small breed who thoroughly enjoyed curling up next to a Deerhound on the sofa, resting a head comfortably on a warm, grey hairy mass. In dog ownership, proper management

### DOGS, DOGS, GOOD FOR YOUR HEART!

People usually purchase dogs for companionship, but studies show that dogs can help to improve their owners' health and level of activity, as well as lower a human's risk of coronary heart disease. Without even realising it, when a person puts time into exercising, grooming and feeding a dog, he also puts more time into his own personal health care. Dog owners establish more routine schedules for their dogs to follow, which can have positive effects on a human's health. Dogs also teach us patience, offer unconditional love and provide the joy of having a furry friend to pet!

Deerhounds generally get on very well with other dogs if they have been properly socialised. This Deerhound's dinner guest is a long-haired Dachshund.

and sensible control play large parts in the success or failure of a relationship.

Many Deerhounds are reputed to chase cats, and to kill them if given half the chance. Again, there are exceptions, and if carefully introduced a hound will live, as mine have, in company with the family cat. Whether or not that same Deerhound would look so favourably on a strange cat crossing his garden path might be quite another matter! With my even-tempered Deerhounds, I even kept a pet Angora rabbit, but never, never would I let the rabbit meet a sighthound nose to nose!

## DEERHOUNDS WITH CHILDREN

Anyone whose dogs come into close contact with children must be sure that each treats the other with respect. This is of particular importance in the case of a dog as large as a Deerhound who could undoubtedly do damage to a child, albeit in error or in play. Children can often engage dogs in their games, encouraging them to become unruly and over-excited. This might be good fun while it lasts, but a quick and unexpected upward movement of a Deerhound's head can all too easily do damage, or a Deerhound jumping up can easily knock over a child.

Deerhounds are tolerant animals and most of them enjoy the company of children, especially if they have been sensibly introduced while the dog is still young. Nevertheless, like all dogs, Deerhounds do appreciate some peace and quiet,

## DO YOU WANT TO LIVE LONGER?

If you like to volunteer, it is wonderful if you can take your dog to a nursing home once a week for several hours. The elder community loves to have a dog with which to visit, and often your dog will bring a bit of companionship to someone who is lonely or somewhat detached from the world. You will be not only bringing happiness to someone else but also keeping your dog busy—and we haven't even mentioned the fact that it has been discovered that volunteering helps to increase your own longevity!

and the limits of their tolerance should never be put to the test.

### LIFESPAN

In general, large breeds do not live so long as smaller ones, so owners should not expect a Deerhound to live well into its teens. Indeed, there are a few that do, but ten or eleven years is a good age for a Deerhound and sadly there are some who don't make it into double figures.

### COAT AND COLOUR

Although it should not be over-coated, the Deerhound is a shaggy-coated breed. The coat is thick, lying close to the body, ragged and harsh or crisp to the touch. Deerhound coats do vary

Although very gentle, Deerhounds are large, strong dogs and probably too much for a child to handle alone. Parents must supervise interaction very closely at all times.

though, and some need more attention than others.

Ideally the coat should be roughly 8 cms (3 ins) to 10 cms (4 ins) long on body, neck and quarters, but the coat on head, breast and belly is substantially softer. The hair on the ear is different again, this described as soft, glossy and like a mouse's coat to the touch. On the inside of both fore- and hindlegs, there is a slightly hairy fringe.

The colour of Deerhounds today seems to have somewhat less variety than in days gone by, when one reads of several light-coloured hounds. Today, the majority of Deerhounds are dark blue-grey, but they may also be darker or lighter grey. In theory they may also be brindle, yellow, sandy red or red fawn with black points, but certainly the paler colours are almost never seen today.

The Deerhound is really a self-coloured dog, so the less white carried in the coat the better. However, a white chest, white toes and a slight white tip to the stern are permissible. Any evidence of a white blaze on the head or a white collar is unacceptable within the breed, and in the United States will disqualify the dog from conformation competition.

## SPEED LIMIT

Because of the Deerhound's size and construction, they can move at great speed; this should always be remembered when exercising off the lead. Young hounds should never be over-exercised until their period of fastest growth is complete, but an adult can readily cope with several miles each day. A combination of lead work on a hard surface coupled with free exercise should be given, and if this can be done twice a day, all the better!

The Deerhound is biddable, but should be trained early, for sadly there are frequent examples of Deerhounds having been

The Deerhound's great speed and keen sighthound instincts make them well suited to racing and lure coursing—activities that provide great exercise and opportunity to hone their natural abilities.

Deerhounds are active participants in activities around the home. Author Juliette Cunliffe with her Deerhound Jemma, who enjoyed helping with the chores of rural life.

injured or even killed when they have taken off at speed and are out of sight of their owners.

## HEALTH CONSIDERATIONS

Compared with many other breeds, the Deerhound is a fundamentally healthy one, although like all dogs, some do suffer from illness. It is only fair to owners, and to the dogs themselves, that attention is paid to these. Veterinary research has made great strides in recent years, so owners and breeders are now more aware of problems than they were in years gone by. Knowing something about the problems that may possibly arise can assist owners in knowing what to discuss with breeders and when it will be necessary to seek veterinary advice.

### SENSITIVITY TO ANAESTHETICS

Deerhounds, like other sighthounds, have a low proportion of body fat in relation to their size. As a result, anaesthesia is one of various medications to

> **DID YOU KNOW?**
>
> At the first sign of any minor infection, live yoghurt, administered orally, can be of great benefit. This sometimes has the effect of rectifying the problem almost immediately, before a course of antibiotics becomes necessary. Feeding live yoghurt for several weeks will also usually help the situation if your Deerhound is prone to passing unpleasant wind!

which they are sensitive, so it is important to discuss this with your veterinary surgeon prior to surgery taking place.

A special anaesthetic that is more suitable for Deerhounds and other similar breeds can be used. This avoids the risk of the anaesthetic's recycling through the body, something that can have fatal results, as the author knows, sadly, only too well.

### BLOOD PRESSURE AND HEART

Blood pressure tests have provided data that Deerhounds have the highest blood pressure among the sighthound breeds. In some cases, dogs with high blood pressure suffer from dilated cardiomyopathy, a heart problem in which the heart muscle becomes feeble. This may result in poor ability to exercise, coughing, fainting, collapse or heart failure. This does occur in Deerhounds, but is not so commonly seen as in some other large breeds. The additive L-carnitine has proved helpful with dilated cardiomyopathy and this should be discussed with your vet.

### LIVER SHUNT

All Deerhound litters should be tested for liver shunt in order to detect any affected puppies. Liver shunt is a non-inflammatory disorder that is a result of abnormal blood vessel develop-ment before birth. It produces signs similar to liver failure and is apparent in youngsters.

This problem causes liver cells to be deprived of nutrients needed to synthesise plasma proteins and other substances, hampering growth. High concentrations of ammonia remain in the blood and these high levels can affect the brain. Signs of the disease are vomiting, loss of appetite, convulsions and other mental disturbance.

### BONE CANCER

Bone cancer more commonly affects larger breeds than smaller ones and has been cited in Deerhounds. Unfortunately, most tumours involving bone are malignant, and tumours occur particularly at the ends of the long bones. Initial signs are evident pain and lameness, with or without localised swelling.

### WEIGHT AND GASTRIC TORSION

Deerhounds rarely become grossly overweight, but it is essential to remember that they should never be fed within an hour, before or after, of exercise for this can cause serious veterinary problems. Commonly affecting deep-chested breeds, gastric torsion, also known as bloat or gastric dilatation, is a rapid accumulation of gas and liquid in the stomach of a dog. This accumulation distends the stomach, leading to blockage of the sphincter. The stomach can also become displaced, twisting in on itself, again blocking the sphincter. This can be fatal, so veterinary attention must be sought as a matter of urgency. Surgery can be successful, but regrettably the post-operative death rate is quite high.

The initial sign is a distended abdomen with copious salivation, and unproductive attempts to vomit. Respiratory difficulties ensue, followed by a state of shock. If tapping the abdominal wall creates a drum-like sound, this is indicative of torsion.

### THYROID PROBLEMS

Tests have shown that Deerhounds often have under-active thyroids, which means that the level of the thyroid hormone in the blood is lower than would be expected. However, in Deerhounds this falls within the breed's normal range and does not, therefore, indicate a particularly high incidence of hypothyroidism.

### INJURY

The Deerhound enjoys running and can do so swiftly and often. However, so engrossed is the hound with the excitement of the chase that an accident may happen. Deerhounds used in coursing frequently work on rough terrain. Wire fences are also prone to appear from nowhere!

People who run their Deerhounds loose on territory unknown to them should always be on the alert for mishaps, and remember that it may well be impossible to carry an injured hound to one's vehicle. If ever you do need to leave an injured dog in order to obtain help, make certain the dog is left as warm and comfortable as possible. Carry a first-aid kit for minor abrasions.

### TEETH

Deerhounds have strong teeth, but it is always important to pay close attention to the care of teeth and gums. This way they will remain as healthy as possible with consequent prevention of decay, infection and resultant loss of teeth.

Infection in the gums may not just stop there. The bacteria from such infection is carried through the bloodstream, the result of which can be diseases of the liver, kidney, heart and joints. This is all the more reason to realise that efficient dental care is of the utmost importance throughout any dog's life.

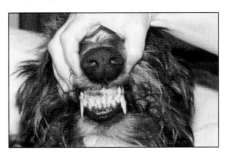

A proper, healthy adult bite. Dental maintenance is just as important as the other aspects of your Deerhound's health care.

# Breed Standard for the

# DEERHOUND

## INTRODUCTION TO THE BREED STANDARD

The breed standard for the Deerhound is set down by The Kennel Club. In England the standard remained virtually unchanged for around 100 years, until it was revised during the 1980s. This was not done at the request of the Deerhound Club, but of The Kennel Club, which at that time changed all breed standards to create some uniformity between them.

Various highly experienced and eminent people within the Deerhound Club were involved in this change, but they were obliged to delete any extraneous words and they were not allowed to stipulate faults. Instead, 'faults' were described as 'undesirable' or 'unacceptable.' Thankfully, because the Deerhound had for so many years been referred to as the 'Highland Greyhound' or 'Rough Coated Greyhound,' The Kennel Club allowed reference to 'a roughcoated greyhound' to remain.

A breed standard is designed effectively to paint a picture in words, though each reader will almost certainly interpret these words slightly differently. However, reading the words alone is never enough to fully comprehend the intricacies of a breed. In addition, it is necessary for devotees to watch other Deerhounds being judged at shows and, if possible, to attend specialist breed seminars. Truly dedicated Deerhound owners will want to give themselves every possible opportunity to absorb as much as possible about the breed they love so much.

In Britain each standard commences with a short section under the heading 'General Appearance,' this giving a short *précis* of what the breed should look like. The second heading for all breeds, titled 'Characteristics,' provides a clear description of what the breed should possess; in the Deerhound this is a unique combination of speed, power and endurance necessary to pull down a stag, with a general bearing of gentle dignity.

Following a description of temperament, each standard goes on to portray various aspects of the breed, serving as a useful

This Deerhound was shown at the 2001 World Dog Show in Porto, Portugal. At this annual show, dogs are judged according to Fédération Internationale Cynologique (FCI) breed standards.

reference. The breed standard undoubtedly helps breeders to produce stock that comes as close to the standard as possible, and helps judges to know exactly what they are looking for. In this way, to head his line of winners, the judge can select the Deerhound that he considers to conform most closely to the breed standard.

However familiar you are with the Deerhound, it is always worth refreshing your memory by re-reading the standard, for it is sometimes too easy to conveniently forget or 'overlook' certain features of the breed.

**BREEDING CONSIDERATIONS**

The decision to breed your dog is one that must be considered carefully and researched thoroughly before moving into action. Some people believe that breeding will make their bitches happier or that it is an easy way to make money. Unfortunately, indiscriminate breeding only worsens the rampant problem of pet overpop-ulation, as well as putting a consider-able dent in your pocketbook. As for the bitch, the entire process from mating through whelping is not an easy one and puts your pet under considerable stress. Last, but not least, consider whether or not you have the means to care for an entire litter of pups. Without a reputation in the field, your attempts to sell the pups may be unsuccessful.

## THE KENNEL CLUB STANDARD FOR THE DEERHOUND

**General Appearance:** Resembles a roughcoated greyhound of larger size and bone.

**Characteristics:** The build suggests the unique combination of speed, power and endurance necessary to pull down a stag, but general bearing is one of gentle dignity.

**Temperament:** Gentle and friendly. Obedient and easy to train because eager to please. Docile and good-tempered, never suspicious, aggressive or nervous. Carries himself with quiet dignity.

**Head and Skull:** Broadest at ears, tapering slightly to eyes, muzzle tapering more decidedly to nose, lips level. Head long, skull flat rather than round, with very slight rise over eyes, with no stop. Skull coated with moderately long hair, softer than rest of coat. Nose slightly aquiline and black. In lighter coloured dogs black muzzle preferred. Good moustache of rather silky hair and some beard.

**Eyes:** Dark. Generally dark brown or hazel. Light eyes undesirable. Moderately full with a soft look in repose, but keen, far away look when dog is roused. Rims black.

This is an excellent example of the Deerhound, helping you visualise the written description set forth in the standard.

Handlers gait their dogs in the ring so that the dogs' movement can be evaluated. This is very important in the Deerhound, as it indicates how well the dog would be able to perform its intended function.

**Ears:** Set on high and in repose folded back. In excitement raised above head without losing the fold and in some cases semi-erect. A big thick ear hanging flat to the head or a prick ear most undesirable. Ear soft, glossy and like a mouse's coat to the touch; the smaller the better, no long coat or fringe. Ears black or dark coloured.

**Mouth:** Jaws strong, with a perfect, regular and complete scissor bite, i.e. upper teeth closely overlapping lower teeth and set square to the jaws.

**Neck:** Very strong with good reach sometimes disguised by mane. Nape of neck very prominent where head is set on, no throatiness.

Dr Seamus Caine's Ch Killoeter Onich won the Hound Group at a Kennel Club show.

**Forequarters:** Shoulders well laid, not too far apart. Loaded and straight shoulders undesirable. Forelegs straight, broad and flat, a good broad forearm and elbow being desirable.

**Body:** Body and general formation that of a greyhound of larger size and bone. Chest deep rather than broad, not too narrow and flat-sided. Loin well arched and drooping to tail. Flat topline undesirable.

**Hindquarters:** Drooping, broad and powerful, hips set wide apart. Hindlegs well bent at stifle with great length from hip to hock. Bone broad and flat.

**Feet:** Compact and well knuckled. Nails strong.

**Tail:** Long, thick at root, tapering and reaching almost to ground. When standing dropped perfectly straight down or curved. Curved when moving, never lifted above line of back. Well covered with hair; on upper side thick and wiry, on under side longer, and towards end a slight fringe is not objectionable. A curl or ring tail undesirable.

**Gait/Movement:** Easy, active and true, with a long stride.

**Coat:** Shaggy, but not overcoated. Woolly coat unacceptable. The correct coat is thick, close-lying, ragged; harsh or crisp to the touch. Hair on body, neck and quarters harsh and wiry about 8 cms (3 ins) to 10 cms (4 ins) long; that on head, breast and belly much softer. A slight hairy fringe on inside of fore- and hindlegs.

**Colour:** Dark blue-grey, darker and lighter greys and brindles and yellows, sandy-red or red fawns with black points. A white chest, white toes and a slight white tip to stern are permissible but the less white the better, since it is a self-coloured dog. A white blaze on head or white collar unacceptable.

**Size:** Height: dogs: minimum desirable height at withers 76 cms (30 ins); bitches: 71 cms (28 ins). Weight: dogs: about 45.5 kgs (100 lbs); bitches about 36.5 kgs (80 lbs).

**Faults:** Any departure from the foregoing points should be considered a fault and the seriousness with which the fault should be regarded should be in exact proportion to its degree.

**Note:** Male animals should have two apparently normal testicles fully descended into the scrotum.

A sketch of a male Deerhound, showing correct type, balance and proportion.

## THE IDEAL SPECIMEN

According to The Kennel Club, 'The Breed Standard is the "Blueprint" of the ideal specimen in each breed approved by a governing body, e.g. The Kennel Club, the Fédération Cynologique Internationale (FCI) and the American Kennel Club.

'The Kennel Club writes and revises Breed Standards taking account of the advice of Breed Councils/Clubs. Breed Standards are not changed lightly to avoid "changing the standard to fit the current dogs" and the health and well-being of future dogs is always taken into account when new standards are prepared or existing ones altered.'

The body illustrations below show faults in the Deerhound.

Flat topline; incorrect ring tail with improper high set and carriage; straight, weak rear; short neck.

Deerhound head in which the foreface is too short, lacking strength and substance. The topskull is domed and the stop too pronounced.

'East-west' front; shallow brisket; weak, underdeveloped tucked-under rear.

Long back, flat topline and lack of arch over loin. However, this dog does possess a strong sloping rear that provides proper propulsion.

Deerhound head of correct proportions, with correct ear size and carriage.

Straight shoulders; weak pasterns; shallow chest; extreme arch over loin; dip behind shoulders; weak, under-angulated rear.

Compare this Irish Wolfhound head, which is generally stronger and more substantial.

## *Your Puppy*

# DEERHOUND

### HOW TO SELECT A PUPPY

Before deciding to look for a Deerhound puppy, it is essential that you fully appreciate the merits and drawbacks of the breed. You must be absolutely clear in your mind that this is the right breed for you and your family. Apart from other aspects of the breed, you will have to take into consideration size and strength, temperament, exercise, feeding and housing.

You may also wish to consider taking out veterinary insurance, for vet's bills can mount up, especially for a large dog. You must always be certain that sufficient funds are available to give your dog any veterinary attention that may be needed.

You must select a puppy from a caring breeder who has given the puppies all the attention they deserve, and has looked after them well. A young puppy should look well-fed, but not pot-bellied, as this might indicate worms. Take note of eyes that should look bright and clear, without discharge. Nor, of course, should there be any discharge from the nose, and certainly no evidence of loose motions. It goes without saying that the puppies should all be clean, with absolutely no evidence of parasites such as fleas or lice. Always check the bite of

> **PUPPY SELECTION**
>
> Your selection of a good puppy can be determined by your needs. A show potential or a good pet? It is your choice. Every puppy, however, should be of good temperament. Although show-quality puppies are bred and raised with emphasis on physical conformation, responsible breeders strive for equally good temperament. Do not buy from a breeder who concentrates solely on physical beauty at the expense of personality.

your selected puppy to be sure that it is neither overshot nor undershot. This may not be too noticeable on a young puppy, but will become more evident as the puppy gets older. The Deerhound should have a perfect scissor bite.

It is essential that you select a breeder with the utmost care. Initially The Kennel Club will be able to put you in contact with a

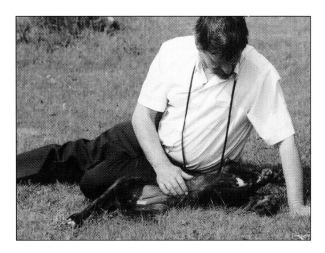

An eleven-week old puppy, enjoying a bit of fuss!

## PREPARING FOR PUP

Unfortunately, when a puppy is bought by someone who does not take into consideration the time and attention that dog ownership requires, it is the puppy who suffers when he is either abandoned or placed in a shelter by a frustrated owner. So all of the 'homework' you do in preparation for your pup's arrival will benefit you both. The more informed you are, the more you will know what to expect and the better equipped you will be to handle the ups and downs of raising a puppy. Hopefully, everyone in the household is willing to do his part in raising and caring for the pup. The anticipation of owning a dog often brings a lot of promises from excited family members: 'I will walk him every day,' 'I will feed him,' 'I will house-train him,' etc., but these things take time and effort, and promises can easily be forgotten once the novelty of the new pet has worn off.

breed club, or perhaps directly with breeders, but it is always a good idea to visit a large show at which Deerhounds will be exhibited. This will provide you with a valuable opportunity to meet various breeders and to see the quality of their stock.

Once you have made the initial contact with a breeder or two and decided which breeder is best suited to your needs, it's time to visit the litter. Since you are likely to be choosing a Deerhound as a pet dog and not a show dog, you simply should select a pup that is friendly, attractive and healthy. Deerhounds generally have large litters, averaging eight puppies, so you should have plenty from which to select your pup. Likely there will be both male and female puppies available. There is not a tremendous difference between the sexes in the Deerhound. In terms of

## PUPPY APPEARANCE

Your puppy should have a well-fed appearance but not a distended abdomen, which may indicate worms or incorrect feeding, or both. The body should be firm, with a solid feel. The skin of the abdomen should be pale pink and clean, without signs of scratching or rash. Check the hind legs to make certain that dewclaws were removed, if any were present at birth.

size, it's big versus bigger. Of course the male, as in most breeds, is larger and stronger. Temperamentally, male puppies, at around seven months when they reach sexual maturity, can become 'headstrong' and need to be clearly informed who is the king in your castle.

Breeders commonly allow visitors to see their litters by

around the fifth or sixth week, and puppies leave for their new homes between the eighth and tenth week. Breeders who permit their puppies to leave early are more interested in your pounds than in their puppies' well-being. Puppies need to learn the rules of the pack from their dams, and most dams continue teaching the pups manners and dos and don'ts until around the eighth week. Breeders spend significant amounts of time with the Deerhound toddlers so that the pups are able to interact with the 'other species,' i.e. humans. Given the long history that dogs and humans share, bonding between the two species is natural but must be nurtured. A well-bred, well-socialised Deerhound pup wants nothing more than to be near you and please you.

## COMMITMENT OF OWNERSHIP

After considering all of these factors, you have most likely already made some very important decisions about will help you learn to recognise certain behaviour and to determine what a pup's behaviour indicates about his temperament. You will be able to pick out which pups are the leaders, which ones are less outgoing, confident, shy, playful, friendly, aggressive, etc. Equally as important, you will learn to recognise what an healthy pup should look and act like. All of these things will help you in your search, and when you find the Deerhound that was meant for you, you will know it!

selecting your puppy. You have chosen a Deerhound, which means that you have decided which characteristics you want in a dog and what type of dog will complement your family and lifestyle. If you have selected a breeder, you have gone a step further—you have done your research and found a responsible, conscientious person who breeds quality Deerhounds and who should be a reliable source of help as you and your puppy adjust to life together. If you have observed a litter in action, you have obtained a firsthand look at the dynamics of a puppy 'pack' and, thus, you have learned about each pup's individual personality— perhaps you have even found one that particularly appeals to you.

However, even if you have not yet found the Deerhound puppy of your dreams, observing pups

Eleven-week-old puppy bitch 'Lottie,' bred by Glenis Peach, with Mick Peach. Lottie soon came to be owned by the author in partnership with Carol Ann Johnson.

## DOCUMENTATION

Two important documents you will get from the breeder are the pup's pedigree and registration certificate. The breeder should register the litter and each pup with The Kennel Club, and it is necessary for you to have the paperwork if you plan on showing or breeding in the future.

Make sure you know the breeder's intentions on which type of registration he will obtain for the pup. There are limited registrations which may prohibit the dog from being shown, bred or competing in non-conformation trials such as Working or Agility if the breeder feels that the pup is not of sufficient quality to do so. There is also a type of registration that will permit the dog in non-conformation competition only.

On the reverse side of the registration certificate, the new owner can find the transfer section, which must be signed by the breeder.

## PREPARING PUPPY'S PLACE IN YOUR HOME

Researching your breed and finding a breeder are only two aspects of the 'homework' you will have to do before taking your Deerhound puppy home. You will also have to prepare your home and family for the new addition. Much as you would prepare a nursery for a newborn baby, you will need to designate a place in your home that will be the puppy's own. How you prepare your home will depend on how much freedom the dog will be allowed. Whatever you decide, you must ensure that he has a place that he can 'call his own.'

When you bring your new puppy into your home, you are bringing him into what will become his home as well. Obviously, you did not buy a puppy with the intentions of catering to his every whim and allowing him to 'rule the roost,' but in order for a puppy to grow into a stable, well-adjusted dog, he has to feel comfortable in his surroundings. Remember, he is leaving the warmth and security

## INSURANCE

Many good breeders will offer you insurance with your new puppy, which is an excellent idea. The first few weeks of insurance will probably be covered free of charge or with only minimal cost, allowing you to take up the policy when this expires. If you own a pet dog, it is sensible to take out such a policy as veterinary fees can be high, although routine vaccinations and boosters are not covered. Look carefully at the many options open to you before deciding which suits you best.

of his mother and littermates, as well as the familiarity of the only place he has ever known, so it is important to make his transition as easy as possible. By preparing a place in your home for the puppy, you are making him feel as welcome as possible in a strange new place. It should not take him long to get used to it, but the sudden shock of being transplanted is somewhat traumatic for a young pup. Imagine how a small child would feel in the same situation—that is how your puppy must be feeling. It is up to you to reassure him and to let him know, 'Little tyke, you are going to like it here!'

## WHAT YOU SHOULD BUY

### CRATE
Most breeders do not recommend the Deerhound to be crate-trained, though there are definite merits to

having the dog acclimated to a crate. To someone unfamiliar with the use of crates in dog training, it may seem like punishment to shut a dog in a crate, but this is not the case at all. Although all breeders do not advocate crate training, some breeders and trainers are recommending crates as preferred tools for show puppies as well as pet puppies.

Crate training is becoming the preferred means of house-training a puppy and provides your dog with a safe means by which to travel by car (or plane). All dogs, regardless of size, need a place of their own in the home. The crate serves as a 'doggie bedroom' of sorts—your Deerhound puppy can curl up in his crate when he wants to sleep or when he just needs a break. During house-training, puppies sleep in their crates overnight and spend time there when not supervised. With soft bedding and his favourite toy, a crate becomes a cosy pseudo-

Puppies should be friendly and inquisitive, as is this young Deerhound who introduces himself to a visiting relative.

den for your dog.

Likely, your Deerhound will not use his crate very much after you have completed the toilet-training process; nonetheless, it is a very effective mechanism to instil clean habits in the Deerhound.

As far as purchasing a crate, the type that you buy is up to you. It will most likely be one of the two most popular types: wire or fibreglass. There are advantages and disadvantages to each type. For example, a wire crate is more open, allowing the air to flow

Your local pet shop will have a wide array of crates from which you may choose the one which best suits your needs.

PHOTO COURTESY OF DOSKOCIL.

through and affording the dog a view of what is going on around him, while a fibreglass crate is sturdier and required for airplane travel. Both can double as travel crates for your vehicle, providing safety and protection for the dog. It's wise to purchase the largest crate possible for the Deerhound. Your pet-supply outlet may have this in stock, or the store may have to special-order it.

### BEDDING
Veterinary bedding in the dog's crate will help the dog feel more

heat and something with which to snuggle. You will want to wash your pup's bedding frequently in case he has a toileting 'accident' in his crate, and replace or remove any blanket that becomes ragged and starts to fall apart.

### TOYS

Toys are a must for dogs of all ages, especially for curious playful pups. Puppies are the 'children' of the dog world, and what child does not love toys? Chew toys provide enjoyment for both dog and owner—your dog will enjoy playing with his favourite toys, while you will enjoy the fact that they distract him from chewing on your expensive shoes and leather sofa.

Puppies love to chew; in fact, chewing is a physical need for pups as they are teething, and everything looks appetising! The full range of your possessions— from old tea towel to Oriental carpet—are fair game in the eyes of a teething pup. Puppies are not all that discerning when it comes to finding something literally to 'sink their teeth into'—everything tastes great! Deerhound puppies are chewers, but as adults they do not tend to chew unless they are bored.

Deerhounds should play only with large balls, for their mouths are large and small balls could be swallowed. They enjoy large marrow bones; these are

at home, and you may also like to pop in a small blanket. First, this will take the place of the leaves, twigs, etc., that the pup would use in the wild to make a den; the pup can make his own 'burrow' in the crate. Although your pup is far removed from his den-making ancestors, the denning instinct is still a part of his genetic makeup. Second, until you take your pup home, he has been sleeping amidst the warmth of his mother and littermates, and while a blanket is not the same as a warm, breathing body, it still provides

## CRATE TRAINING TIPS

During crate training, you should partition off the section of the crate in which the pup stays. If he is given too big an area, this will hinder your training efforts. Crate training is based on the fact that a dog does not like to soil his sleeping quarters, so it is ineffective to keep a pup in a crate that is so big that he can eliminate in one end and get far enough away from it to sleep. Also, you want to make the crate den-like for the pup. Blankets and a favourite toy will make the crate cosy for the small pup; as he grows, you may want to evict some of his 'roommates' to make more room.

It will take some coaxing at first, but be patient. Given some time to get used to it, your pup will adapt to his new home-within-a-home quite nicely.

especially useful for loosening puppies' baby teeth. Although they like rawhide chews, these must be of the very largest kind (and not with knots on the end), for small ones are likely to be swallowed whole. If hide chews are given, for safety's sake they must be removed when they start to wear down to smaller size.

Sticks and natural bones can be highly dangerous for dogs. Never allow your Deerhound to play with these. Provide him safe chew toys that will not splinter or break in the Deerhound's very powerful jaws.

### LEAD

A nylon lead is probably the best option, as it is the most resistant to puppy teeth should your pup take a liking to chewing on his lead. Of course, this is a habit that should be nipped in the bud, but, if your pup likes to chew on his lead, he has a very slim chance of being able to chew through the strong nylon. Nylon leads are also lightweight, which is good for a young Deerhound who is just getting used to the idea of walking on a lead.

For everyday walking and safety purposes, the nylon lead is a good choice. As your pup grows up and gets used to walking on the lead, you will want to purchase a flexible lead to give your sighthound more freedom to trot along. These leads allow you

## TOYS, TOYS, TOYS!

With a big variety of dog toys available, and so many that look like they would be a lot of fun for a dog, be careful in your selection. It is amazing what a set of puppy teeth can do to an innocent-looking toy, so, obviously, safety is a major consideration. Be sure to choose the most durable products that you can find. Hard nylon bones and toys are a safe bet, and many of them are offered in different scents and

flavours that will be sure to capture your dog's attention. It is always fun to play a game of catch with your dog, and there are balls and flying discs that are specially made to withstand dog teeth.

to extend the length to give the dog a broader area to explore or to shorten the length to keep the dog near you.

### COLLAR

Your pup should get used to wearing a collar all the time since you will want to attach his ID tags to it; plus, you have to attach the lead to something! A lightweight nylon collar is a good choice. Make certain that the collar fits snugly enough so that the pup cannot wriggle out of it, but is loose enough so that it will not be uncomfortably tight around the pup's neck. You should be able to fit a finger between the pup's neck and the collar. It may take some time for your pup to get used to wearing the collar, but soon he

will not even notice that it is there. Choke collars are made for training, but can damage the Deerhound's coat and are not recommended for use with this breed.

A young Deerhound models a sturdy yet lightweight collar attached to a light leather lead.

Your local pet shop sells an array of dishes and bowls for water and food.

PHOTO COURTESY OF MIKKI PET PRODUCTS.

## FOOD AND WATER BOWLS

Your pup will need two bowls, one for food and one for water. You may want two sets of bowls, one for indoors and one for outdoors, depending on where the dog will be fed and where he will be spending time. Stainless steel or sturdy plastic bowls are popular choices. Plastic bowls are more chewable, but dogs tend not to chew on the steel variety, which can be sterilised. It is important to buy sturdy bowls since anything is in danger of being chewed by puppy teeth and you do not want your dog to be constantly chewing apart his bowl (for his safety and for your purse!). You will also want to invest in a double-bowl stand to elevate your Deerhound's food and water bowls. Deep-chested

### FINANCIAL RESPONSIBILITY

Grooming tools, collars, leashes, dog beds and, of course, toys will be an expense to you when you first obtain your pup, and the cost will continue throughout your dog's lifetime. If your puppy damages or destroys your possessions (as most puppies surely will!) or something belonging to a neighbour, you can calculate additional expense. There is also flea and pest control, which every dog owner faces more than once. You must be able to handle the financial responsibility of owning a dog.

# CHOOSE AN APPROPRIATE COLLAR

The **BUCKLE COLLAR** is the standard collar used for everyday purposes. Be sure that you adjust the buckle on growing puppies. Check it every day. It can become too tight overnight! These collars can be made of leather or nylon. Attach your dog's identification tags to this collar.

The **CHOKE COLLAR** is made for training, though the chain choke is too harsh on the Deerhound's coat. It is constructed of highly polished steel so that it slides easily through the stainless steel loop. The idea is that the dog controls the pressure around its neck and he will stop pulling if the collar becomes uncomfortable. It should *only* be used during training and never left on the dog.

The **HALTER** is for a trained dog that has to be restrained to prevent running away, chasing a cat and the like. Considered the most humane of all collars, it is frequently used on smaller dogs for which collars are not comfortable.

It is your respon-
sibility to clean
up after your
Deerhound has
relieved itself. Pet
shops have
various aids to
assist in the
clean-up job.

breeds like the Deerhound should never crane their necks when they are eating or drinking, as this may be a possible instigator of bloat.

### CLEANING SUPPLIES

Until a pup is house-trained, you will be doing a lot of cleaning. 'Accidents' will occur, which is acceptable in the beginning stages of toilet training because the puppy does not know any better. All you can do is be prepared to clean up any accidents as soon as they happen. Old rags, towels, newspapers and a safe disinfectant are good to have on hand.

### BEYOND THE BASICS

The items previously discussed are the bare necessities. You will find out what else you need as you go along—grooming supplies, flea/tick protection, baby gates to

partition a room, etc. These things will vary depending on your situation, but it is important that you have everything you need to feed and make your Deerhound comfortable in his first few days at home.

### PUPPY-PROOFING YOUR HOME

Aside from making sure that your Deerhound will be comfortable in your home, you also have to make sure that your home is safe for your Deerhound. This means taking precautions that your pup will not get into anything he should not get into and that there is nothing within his reach that may harm him should he sniff it, chew it, inspect it, etc. This probably seems obvious since, while you are primarily concerned with your pup's safety, at the same time you do not want your belongings to be ruined. Breakables should be placed out of reach if your dog is to have full run of the house. If he is to be limited to certain places within the house, keep any potentially dangerous items in the 'off-limits' areas.

An electrical cord can pose a danger should the puppy decide to taste it—and who is going to convince a pup that it would not make a great chew toy? Cords should be fastened tightly against the wall. If your dog is going to spend time in a crate, make sure that there is nothing near his crate that he can reach if he sticks his curious little nose or paws through the openings. Just as you would with a child, keep all household cleaners and chemicals where the pup cannot reach them.

It is also important to make sure that the outside of your home is safe. Of course, your puppy should never be unsupervised, but a pup let loose in the garden will want to run and explore, and he should be granted that freedom. Do not let a

fence give you a false sense of security; you would be surprised at how crafty (and persistent) a dog can be in working out how to dig under and squeeze his way through small holes, or to jump or climb over a fence.

While most Deerhounds are not diggers, bitches may develop the habit after their oestrus.

Lottie, pictured here at 14 weeks old, looks like she's about to do some gardening!

Jumping, however, is another story, and when an 81-cm (32-inch) sighthound likes to jump, you better pay attention. It's required that your fence be at least 2 metres high in order to keep the Deerhound safely within its confines. Once a Deerhound has cleared a fence, you can be certain that this natural 'wind merchant' is going to fly—and catching him will be a task for an army of dog patrolmen.

### FIRST TRIP TO THE VET

The breeder of your Deerhound puppy can likely recommend a qualified vet in your area, someone who knows large breeds or sighthounds, or maybe you know some other Deerhound owners who can suggest a good vet. Either way, you should have an appointment arranged for your pup before you pick him up.

The pup's first visit will consist of an overall examination to make sure that the pup does not have any problems that are not apparent to you. The veterinary surgeon will also set up a schedule for the pup's vaccinations; the breeder will inform you of which ones the pup has already received and the vet can continue from there.

### INTRODUCTION TO THE FAMILY

Everyone in the house will be excited about the puppy's coming

home and will want to pet him and play with him, but it is best to make the introduction low-key so as not to overwhelm the puppy. He is apprehensive already. It is the first time he has been separated from his mother and the breeder, and the ride to your home is likely to be the first time he has been in a car. The last thing you want to do is smother him, as this will only frighten him further. This is not to say that human contact is not extremely necessary at this stage, because this is the time when a connection between the pup and his human family is formed. Gentle petting and soothing words should help console him, as well as just putting him down and letting him explore on his own (under your watchful eye, of course).

The pup may approach the

It's dinner for two for Lottie and litter brother Lucky, pictured at 11 weeks old.

family members or may busy himself with exploring for a while. Gradually, each person should spend some time with the pup, one at a time, crouching down to get as close to the pup's level as possible, letting him sniff their hands and petting him gently. He definitely needs human attention and he needs to be touched—this is how to form an immediate bond. Just remember that the pup is experiencing many things for the first time, at the same time. There are new people, new noises, new smells and new things to investigate, so be gentle, be affectionate and be as comforting as you can be.

## PUP'S FIRST NIGHT HOME

You have travelled home with your new charge safely in his crate. He's been to the vet for a thorough check-up; he's been weighed, his papers have been examined and perhaps he's even been vaccinated and wormed as well. He's met (and licked!) the whole family, including the excited children and the less-than-happy cat. He's explored his area, his new bed, the garden and anywhere else he's been permitted. He's eaten his first meal at home and relieved himself in the proper place. He's heard lots of new sounds, smelled new friends and seen more of the outside world than ever before... and that was just the first day! He's worn out and is ready for bed...or so you think!

It's puppy's first night home and you are ready to say 'Good night.' Keep in mind that this is his first night ever to be sleeping alone. His dam and littermates are no longer at paw's length and he's a bit scared, cold and lonely. Be reassuring to your new family member, but this is not the time to spoil him and give in to his inevitable whining.

Puppies whine to let others know where they are and hopefully to get company out of it. Place your pup in his new bed or crate in his designated area and close the door. Mercifully, he may fall asleep without a peep. When the inevitable occurs, however, ignore the whining—-he is fine. Be strong and keep his interest in mind. Do not allow yourself to

### THE RIDE HOME

Taking your dog from the breeder to your home in a car can be a very uncomfortable experience for both of you. The puppy will have been taken from his warm, friendly, safe environment and brought into a strange new environment—an environment that moves! Be prepared for loose bowels, urination, crying, whining and even fear biting. With proper love and encouragement when you arrive home, the stress of the trip should quickly disappear.

feel guilty and visit the pup. He will fall asleep eventually.

Many breeders recommend placing a piece of bedding from the pup's former home in his new bed so that he recognises and is comforted by the scent of his littermates. Others still advise placing a hot water bottle in the bed for warmth. The latter may be a good idea provided the pup doesn't attempt to suckle—he'll get good and wet, and may not fall asleep so fast.

Puppy's first night can be somewhat stressful for both the pup and his new family. Remember that you are setting the tone of night-time at your house. Unless you want to play with your pup every night at 10 p.m., midnight and 2 a.m., don't initiate the habit. Your family will thank you, and so will your pup!

## PREVENTING PUPPY PROBLEMS

### SOCIALISATION

Now that you have done all of the preparatory work and have helped your pup get accustomed to his new home and family, it is about time for you to have some fun! Socialising your Deerhound pup gives you the opportunity to show off your new friend, and your pup gets to reap the benefits of being an adorable furry creature that people will want to pet and, in general, think is

---

**PUPPY PROBLEMS**

The majority of problems that are commonly seen in young pups will disappear as your dog gets older. However, how you deal with problems when he is young will determine how he reacts to discipline as an adult dog. It is important to establish who is boss (hopefully it will be you!) right away when you are first bonding with your dog. This bond will set the tone for the rest of your life together.

---

absolutely precious!

Besides getting to know his new family, your puppy should be exposed to other people, animals and situations. This will help him become well adjusted as he grows up and less prone to being timid or fearful of the new things he will encounter. Of course, he must not come into close contact with dogs you don't know well until his course of injections is fully complete.

Your pup's socialisation began with the breeder, but now it is your responsibility to continue it. The socialisation he receives until the age of 12 weeks is the most critical, as this is the time when he forms his impressions of the outside world. Be especially careful during the eight-to-ten-week-old period, also known as the fear period. The interaction he receives during this time should be gentle and reassuring. Lack of socialisation and/or negative experiences during the socialisation period can manifest itself in fear and aggression as the dog grows up. Your puppy needs lots of positive interaction, which of course includes human contact, affection, handling and exposure to other animals.

Once your pup has received his necessary vaccinations, feel free to take him out and about (on his lead, of course). Walk him around the neighbourhood, take him on your daily errands, let people pet him, let him meet other dogs and pets, etc. Puppies do not have to try to make friends; there will be no shortage of people who will want to introduce themselves. Just make

At 11 weeks of age, puppy Lottie towers over her adult Dachshund friend.

sure that you carefully supervise each meeting. If the neighbourhood children want to say hello, for example, that is great— children and pups most often make great companions. However, sometimes an excited child can unintentionally handle a pup too roughly, or an overzealous pup can playfully nip a little too hard. You want to make socialisation experiences positive ones. What a pup learns during this very formative stage will affect his attitude toward future encounters. You want your dog to be comfortable around everyone. A pup that has a bad experience with a child may grow up to be a dog that is shy around or aggressive toward children.

### CONSISTENCY IN TRAINING

Dogs, being pack animals, naturally need a leader, or else they try to establish dominance in their packs. When you welcome a dog into your family, the choice of who becomes the leader and who becomes the 'pack' is entirely up to you! Your pup's intuitive quest

## MANNERS MATTER

During the socialisation process, a puppy should meet people, experience different environments and definitely be exposed to other canines. Through playing and interacting with other dogs, your puppy will learn lessons, ranging from controlling the pressure of his jaws by biting his littermates to the inner-workings of the canine pack that he will apply to his human relationships for the rest of his life. That is why removing a puppy from its litter too early (before eight weeks) can be detrimental to the pup's development.

for dominance, coupled with the fact that it is nearly impossible to look at an adorable Deerhound pup with his 'puppy-dog' eyes and not cave in, give the pup almost an unfair advantage in getting the upper hand! A pup will definitely test the waters to see what he can and cannot do. Do not give in to those pleading eyes—stand your ground when it comes to disciplining the pup and make sure that all family members do the same. It will only confuse the pup if Mother tells him to get off the sofa when he is used to sitting up there with Father to watch the nightly news. Avoid discrepancies by having all members of the household decide on the rules before the pup even comes home…and be consistent in enforcing them! Early training shapes the dog's personality, so you cannot be unclear in what you expect.

## COMMON PUPPY PROBLEMS

The best way to prevent puppy problems is to be proactive in stopping an undesirable behaviour as soon as it starts. The old saying 'You can't teach an old dog new tricks' does not necessarily hold true, but it is true that it is much easier to discourage bad behaviour in a young developing pup than to wait until the pup's bad behaviour becomes the adult dog's bad habit. There are some problems that are especially prevalent in puppies as they develop.

### NIPPING

As puppies start to teethe, they feel the need to sink their teeth into anything available…unfortunately, that usually includes your fingers, arms, hair and toes. You may find this behaviour cute for the first five seconds…until you feel just how sharp those puppy teeth are. Nipping is something you want to discourage immediately and consistently with a firm 'No!' (or whatever number of firm 'Nos' it takes for him to understand that you mean business). Then, replace your finger with an appropriate chew toy. While this behaviour is merely annoying when the dog is young, it can become dangerous as your Deerhound's adult teeth grow in and his jaws develop, and he continues to think it is okay to gnaw on human appendages. Your Deerhound does not mean any harm with a friendly nip, but he also does not know his own strength.

### CRYING/WHINING

Your pup will often cry, whine, whimper, howl or make some type of commotion when he is left alone. This is basically his way of calling out for attention to make sure that you know he is there and that you have not forgotten about him. Your puppy feels insecure when he is left alone, when you are out of the house and he is in his crate or when you are in another part of the house and he cannot see you. The noise he is making is an expression of the anxiety he feels at being alone, so he needs to be

taught that being alone is okay. You are not actually training the dog to stop making noise; rather, you are training him to feel comfortable when he is alone and thus removing the need for him to make the noise. This is where the crate with cosy bedding and a toy comes in handy. You want to know that your pup is safe when you are not there to supervise, and you know that he will be safe in his crate rather than roaming freely about the house. In order for the pup to stay in his crate without making a fuss, he first needs to be comfortable in his crate. On that note, it is extremely important that the crate is never used as a form of punishment; this will cause the pup to view the crate as a negative place, rather than as a place of his own for safety and retreat.

Accustom the pup to the crate in short, gradually increasing time intervals in which you put him in the crate, maybe with a treat, and stay in the room with him. If he cries or makes a fuss, do not go to him, but stay in his sight. Gradually he will realise that staying in his crate is all right without your help, and it will not be so traumatic for him when you are not around. You may want to leave the radio on softly when you leave the house; the sound of human voices may be comforting to him.

## CHEWING TIPS

Chewing goes hand in hand with nipping in the sense that a teething puppy is always looking for a way to soothe his aching gums. In this case, instead of chewing on you, he may have taken a liking to your favourite shoe or something else which he should not be chewing. Again, realise that this is a normal canine behaviour that does not need to be discouraged, only redirected. Your pup just needs to be taught what is acceptable to chew on and what is off limits. Consistently tell him NO when you catch him chewing on something forbidden and give him a chew toy. Conversely, praise him when you catch him chewing on something appropriate. In this way you are discouraging the inappropriate behaviour and reinforcing the desired behaviour. The puppy chewing should stop after his adult teeth have come in, but an adult dog continues to chew for various reasons—perhaps because he is bored, perhaps to relieve tension or perhaps he just likes to chew. That is why it is important to redirect his chewing when he is still young.

# DEERHOUND

## SPECIAL FEEDING CONSIDERATIONS

Your Deerhound will appreciate feeds at regular times and initially you should be guided by the breeder as to what type of food should be fed and when. When you buy your puppy, the breeder should provide you with a diet sheet giving full details. If you have reason to alter the diet, you will be at liberty to change that food as the youngster matures, but any change should be made gradually.

Knowing what diet works best for dogs of his line, every Deerhound breeder has his own personal preferences regarding the diet for his hounds. Many owners feel it wiser to give their hounds two, or even three, smaller meals each day, rather than just one.

At one time many owners fed fresh meat, including sheep's heads, but with so many good canine foods now available this is no longer necessary. However, there is never any harm in adding a few cooked, diced vegetables to your hound's meal to add a little variety. Always remember that a Deerhound is a large dog with a large appetite.

Owners who choose to feed fresh meat should vary the diet by feeding white meat or fish once or twice a week, as too much red meat can overheat the blood. Whichever diet you choose, it should be carefully balanced and

> **TEST FOR PROPER DIET**
> A good test for proper diet is the colour, odour and firmness of your dog's stool. A healthy dog usually produces three semi-hard stools per day. The stools should have no unpleasant odour. They should be the same colour from excretion to excretion.

should never be too high in protein. Deerhounds that are coursed, though, can cope with a slightly higher protein content.

Because Deerhounds are so tall, as an aid to digestion and to ward off bloat, feeding bowls should be raised from the ground. Specially made feeding accessories are usually available at large dog shows, as these bowl stands may be more difficult to find in a local pet store. Should you be unable to locate a specially designed piece of equipment, you may like to adapt a chair, or something of similar height. The bowl can rest inside the seat space at comfortable eating height.

It is of great importance that your Deerhound is not exercised for at least an hour after feeding, although it may be allowed outside briefly to relieve himself if needed. Also be certain that your Deerhound is not fed following vigorous exercise as this can have ill effects on the dog. After a particularly hectic day, such as at a coursing meeting or a show, your Deerhound should also be given plenty of time to settle down well before food is offered. Always ensure that plenty of water is available at all times.

## TYPES OF FOOD

Today the choices of food for your Deerhound are many and varied. There are simply dozens of brands of food in all sorts of flavours and textures, ranging from puppy diets to those for seniors. There are even hypoallergenic and low-calorie diets available. Because your Deerhound's food has a bearing on coat, health and temperament, it is essential that the most suitable diet is selected for a Deerhound of his age.

Dog foods are produced in three basic types: dried, semi-moist and tinned. Dried foods are useful for the cost-conscious, for overall they tend to be less expensive than semi-moist or tinned foods. Dried foods also contain the least fat and the most preservatives. In general, tinned foods are made up of 60–70 percent water, while semi-moist ones often contain so much sugar that they are perhaps the least preferred by owners, even though their dogs seem to like them.

**FEEDING TIP**
You must store your dried dog food carefully. Open packages of dog food quickly lose their vitamin value, usually within 90 days of being opened. Mould spores and vermin could also contaminate the food.

When selecting your dog's diet, three stages of development must be considered: the puppy stage, the adult stage and the senior or veteran stage.

### PUPPY STAGE

Puppies instinctively want to suck milk from their mother's teats; a normal puppy will exhibit this behaviour just a few moments following birth. If puppies do not attempt to suckle within the first half-hour or so, they should be encouraged to do so by placing them on the nipples, having selected ones with plenty of milk. This early milk supply is important in providing the essential colostrum, which protects the puppies during the first eight to ten weeks of their lives. Although a mother's milk is much better than any milk formula, despite there being some excellent ones available, if the puppies do not feed, the breeder will have to feed them by hand. For those with less experience, advice from a veterinary surgeon is important so that not only the right quantity of milk is fed but also that of correct quality, fed at suitably frequent intervals, usually every two hours during the first few days of life.

Puppies should be allowed to nurse from their mothers for about the first six weeks, although, starting around the third or fourth week, the breeder will begin to introduce small portions of suitable solid food. Most breeders like to introduce alternate milk and meat meals initially, building up to weaning time.

By the time the puppies are seven or a maximum of eight weeks old, they should be fully weaned and fed solely on a proprietary puppy food. Selection of the most suitable, good-quality diet at this time is essential, for a puppy's fastest growth rate is during the first year of life. Veterinary surgeons are usually able to offer advice in this regard. The frequency of meals will be reduced over time, and when a young dog has reached the age of

about 10 months, an adult diet should be fed. Puppy and junior diets should be well balanced for the needs of your dog so that, except in certain circumstances, additional vitamins, minerals and proteins will not be required.

### ADULT DIETS

The Deerhound is physically mature at around 18 months of age and, depending on the food offered, can be changed to an adult diet at about 10 months of age. Again you should rely upon your breeder or veterinary surgeon to recommend an acceptable maintenance diet. Major dog food manufacturers specialise in this

type of food, and it is merely necessary to select the one best suited to your dog's needs. Active dogs have different requirements than sedate dogs. It is important that they do not receive too high a protein content, though coursing dogs can have a little higher content than that for pet and show dogs.

### VETERAN DIETS

As dogs get older, their metabolism changes. The older dog usually exercises less, moves more slowly and sleeps more. This change in lifestyle and physiological performance requires a change in feeding. Since these changes take place slowly, they might not be recognisable.

As the Deerhound becomes less active in its veteran years, usually around six to seven years of age, most owners feed smaller portions instead of changing the actual brand or kind of food. As your dog gets older, few of his organs function up to par. The kidneys slow down and the intestines become less efficient. Be sensitive to your senior Deerhound's diet, as this will help control other problems that may arise with your old friend.

### WATER

Just as your dog needs proper nutrition from his food, water is an essential 'nutrient' as well.

The breeder will have started the pups on a quality puppy food and should provide you with a diet sheet so that you can continue feeding a proper diet.

## DRINK, DRANK, DRUNK— MAKE IT A DOUBLE

In both humans and dogs, as well as most living organisms, water forms the major part of nearly every body tissue. Naturally, we take water for granted, but without it, life as we know it would cease.

For dogs, water is needed to keep their bodies functioning biochemically. Additionally, water is needed to replace the water lost while panting. Unlike humans, who are able to sweat to dissipate heat, dogs must pant to cool down, thereby losing the vital water from their bodies needed to regulate their body temperatures. Humans lose electrolyte-containing products and other body-fluid components through sweating; dogs do not lose anything except water.

Water is essential always, but especially so when the weather is hot or humid or when your dog is exercising or working vigorously.

Water keeps the dog's body properly hydrated and promotes normal function of the body's systems. During house-training, it is necessary to keep an eye on how much water your Deerhound is drinking, but once he is reliably trained he should have access to clean fresh water at all times, especially if you feed dried food. Make certain that the dog's water bowl is clean, and change the water often.

### EXERCISE

Adult Deerhounds certainly need regular exercise and this must be very seriously considered before taking on the breed. It is said that Deerhounds will readily accept as much exercise as their owners wish to give them, and this is very true. One should also bear in mind that, although generally well behaved, adult Deerhounds are very strong so must be trained to walk politely on a lead and not to pull.

However, with regard to youngsters, it is vitally important not to over-exercise a Deerhound puppy, particularly not while its bones are still growing. A puppy should have no more than 20 minutes of lead work each day, and although it will also require free exercise, this should be restricted to a confined area. In a youngster, exercise should be built up slowly.

To keep their limbs and

# What are you feeding your dog?

Read the label on your dog food. Many dog foods only advise what 50—55% of the contents are, leaving the other 45% in doubt.

Calcium 1.3%
Fatty Acids 1.6%
Crude Fibre 4.6%
Moisture 11%
Crude Fat 14%
Crude Protein 22%
**45.5% ? ? ?**

## EXERCISE ALERT!

You should be careful where you exercise your dog. Many country-side areas have been sprayed with chemicals that are highly toxic to both dogs and humans. Never allow your dog to eat grass or drink from puddles on either public or private grounds, as the run-off water may contain chemicals from sprays and herbicides.

muscles in fit condition, Deerhounds should be exercised on a combination of surfaces. Lead work should be done, at least in part, on a hard surface, such as along a country lane or on a paved road. Coupled with this, free exercise is needed on softer ground. It is of great importance always to remember that your Deerhound should never be fed immediately following strenuous exercise, and that after exercise he should be allowed to relax

thoroughly in comfortably warm conditions.

## GROOMING

Deerhounds are rarely, if ever, bathed, but a certain amount of 'tidying up' is done to the coat. However, one must always remember that this is a rough-coated breed, and as such the coat is shaggy. Different people choose to tidy their hounds' coats to a greater or lesser extent, but this is not a breed that should end up looking 'sculptured' in any way!

The coat of the Deerhound does not shed very much, but it does tangle somewhat, so an occasional comb-through with a wide-toothed comb is needed.

The coat on the ear should be like that of a mouse, and to

## GROOMING EQUIPMENT

How much grooming equipment you purchase will depend on how much grooming you are going to do. Here are some basics:
• Natural bristle brush
• Slicker brush
• Metal comb
• Scissors
• Blaster
• Rubber mat
• Dog shampoo
• Spray hose attachment
• Ear cleaner
• Cotton wipes
• Towels
• Nail clippers

## PEDICURE TIP

A dog that spends a lot of time outside on a hard surface, such as cement or pavement, will have his nails naturally worn down and may not need to have them trimmed as often, except maybe in the colder months when he is not outside as much. Regardless, it is best to get your dog accustomed to the nail-trimming procedure at an early age so that he is used to it. Some dogs are especially sensitive about having their feet touched, but if a dog has experienced it since puppyhood, it should not bother him.

emphasise the appearance of neatness and smallness of size of ear, long hairs are usually removed, especially on show dogs. Another area that sometimes needs attention is the foot, as it must look compact. Any hairs distracting from the shape of the foot should be carefully tidied.

On the subject of feet, it is of

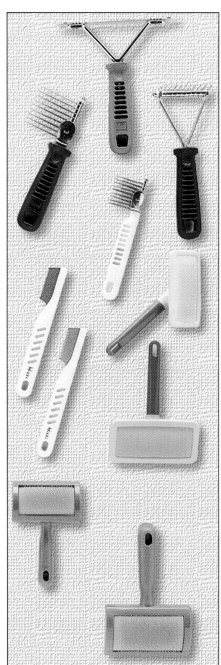

Your local pet shop should have an assortment of grooming items from which you can select the best tools for maintaining your Deerhound's coat.

PHOTO COURTESY OF MIKKI PET PRODUCTS.

## Nail Maintenance

Nail Casing

Quick

Cut Line

**Dark-Coloured Nails**

With black or dark nails, it's best to clip only the tip of the nail or to use a file.

**Light-Coloured Nails**

In light-coloured nails, clipping is much simpler because you can see the vein (or quick) that grows inside the casing.

great importance that nails are kept in trim. The feet of a Deerhound are to be well knuckled, and long nails will cause the toes to splay out. A Deerhound's nails are strong, but this can make them difficult to keep in trim without the right equipment. For Deerhounds, I have found that canine nail clippers of the guillotine type are far more efficient than those with straight edges. Do take care not to cut the quick, for this will be painful and cause bleeding. If ever bleeding does accidentally occur, this can easily be stemmed using potassium permanganate. This is available from your vet, so it is always worth keeping a small supply in your cupboard; in an emergency, household flour apparently will have a similar effect.

It is important, too, that eyes and ears are always kept clean; although Deerhounds do not seem to suffer greatly from dirty ears or eyes, they should still be checked regularly and cleansed accordingly. Check particularly for any build-up of wax in the ear, often detected by an unpleasant smell, but never delve too deeply into the ear, as this could cause injury within the canal.

### BATHING

Again, bathing the Deerhound is only done rarely, but it is something to which the dog

**DEADLY DECAY**
Did you know that periodontal disease (a condition of the bone and gums surrounding a tooth) can be fatal? Having your dog's teeth and mouth checked yearly can prevent it.

should be accustomed as a puppy. You want your dog to be at ease in the bath or else it could end up a wet, soapy, messy ordeal for both of you!

Brush your Deerhound thoroughly before wetting his coat. This will get rid of any mats and tangles, which are harder to remove when the coat is wet. Make certain that your dog has a good non-slip surface on which to stand. Begin by wetting the dog's coat, checking the water temperature to make sure that it is neither too hot nor too cold. A shower or hose attachment is necessary for thoroughly wetting and rinsing the coat.

Next, apply shampoo to the

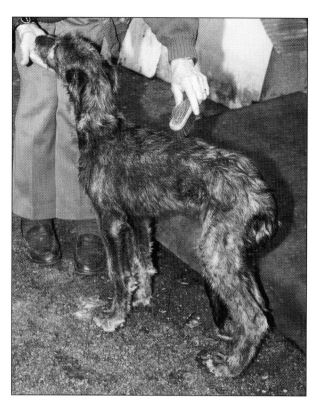

The puppy is introduced to grooming at a young age. This grooming tool has a bristle brush on one side and a pin brush on the other.

dog's coat and work it into a good lather. Wash the head last, as you do not want shampoo to drip into the dog's eyes while you are washing the rest of his body. You should use only a shampoo that is made for dogs. Do not use a product made for human hair. Work the shampoo all the way down to the skin. You can use this opportunity to check the skin for any bumps, bites or other abnormalities. Do not neglect any area of the body—get all of the hard-to-reach places.

Once the dog has been

**NAIL FILING**
You can purchase an electric tool to grind down a dog's nails rather than cut them. Some dogs don't seem to mind the electric grinder but will object strongly to nail clippers. Talking it over with your veterinary surgeon will help you make the right choice.

A wide-toothed metal comb and a pin brush (inset) are recommended for grooming the Deerhound. A thorough once-over on a regular basis will remove any mats, tangles and debris.

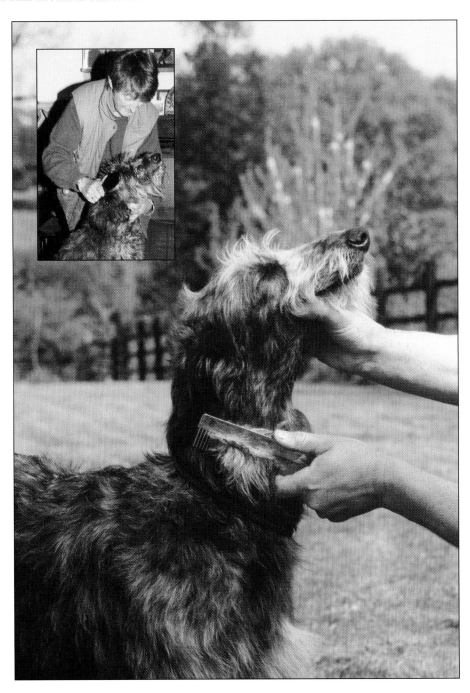

thoroughly shampooed, he requires an equally thorough rinsing. Shampoo left in the coat can be irritating to the dog's skin. Protect his eyes from the shampoo by shielding them with your hand and directing the flow of water in the opposite direction. You should also avoid getting water in the ear canal. Be prepared for your dog to shake out his coat—you might want to stand back, but make sure you have a hold on the dog to keep him from running through the house.

## TRAVELLING WITH YOUR DOG

### CAR TRAVEL

You should accustom your Deerhound to riding in a car at an early age. You may or may not take him in the car often, but at the very least he will need to go to the vet and you do not want these trips to be traumatic for the dog or troublesome for you. The safest way for a dog to ride in the car is in a crate. Of course, a Deerhound-sized crate requires a large vehicle to accommodate it. If you do not have a vehicle large enough to hold the crate, then other options for travel should be explored.

A specially made safety harness for dogs, which straps the dog in much like a seat belt, is a possible option. Never let the dog roam loose in the vehicle—this is very dangerous! If you should stop short, your dog can be thrown and injured. If the dog starts climbing on you and pestering you while you are driving, you will not be able to concentrate on the road. It is an unsafe situation for everyone—human and canine.

For long trips, be prepared to stop to let the dog relieve himself. Take with you whatever you need to clean up after him, including some paper kitchen towels and perhaps some old towelling for use should he have a toileting accident in the car or suffer from travel sickness.

### AIR TRAVEL

While it is possible to take a dog on a flight within Britain, this is fairly unusual and advance permission is always required. The dog will be required to travel in a fibreglass crate and you should always check in advance with the airline regarding specific requirements. To help put the dog at ease, give him one of his favourite toys in the crate. Do not feed the dog for at least six hours before the trip in order to minimise his need to relieve himself. However, certain regulations specify that water must always be made available to the dog in the crate.

Make sure your dog is properly identified and that your contact information appears on his ID tags and on his crate.

Animals travel in a different area of the plane than human passengers, so every rule must be strictly followed so as to prevent the risk of getting separated from your dog.

### HOLIDAYS AND BOARDING

So you want to take a family holiday—and you want to include ALL members of the family. You would probably make arrangements for accommodation ahead of time anyway, but this is especially important when travelling with a dog. You do not want to make an overnight stop at the only place around for miles, only to find out that they do not allow dogs. Also, you do not want to reserve a place for your family without confirming that you are travelling with a large dog, because, if it is against their policy, you may end up without a place to stay.

Alternatively, if you are travelling and choose not to bring your Deerhound, you will have to make arrangements for him while you are away. Some options are to take him to a neighbour's house to stay while you are gone, to have a trusted neighbour pop in often or stay at your house or to bring your dog to a reputable boarding kennel. If you choose to board him at a kennel, you should visit in advance to see the facilities provided and where the dogs are kept. Are the dogs' areas spacious and kept clean? Talk to some of the employees and observe how they treat the dogs—do they spend time with the dogs, play

Should you decide not to take your Deerhound on holiday with you, select a well-kept boarding facility with a knowledgeable staff and plenty of room for the dog.

with them, exercise them, etc.? Also find out the kennel's policy on vaccinations and what it requires. This is for all of the dogs' safety, since there is a greater risk of diseases being passed from dog to dog when they are kept together.

## IDENTIFICATION

Your Deerhound is your valued companion and friend. That is why you always keep a close eye on him and you have made sure that he cannot escape from the garden or wriggle out of his collar and run away from you. However, accidents can happen and there may come a time when your dog unexpectedly becomes separated from you. If this unfortunate event should occur, the first thing on your mind will be finding him. Proper identification, including an ID tag, a tattoo and possibly a microchip, will increase the chances of his being returned to you safely and quickly. Discuss the implantation of a microchip with your veterinary surgeon, who should also have information about tattooing.

## IDENTIFICATION OPTIONS

As puppies become more and more expensive, especially those puppies of high quality for showing and/or breeding, they have a greater chance of being stolen. The usual collar dog tag is, of course, easily removed. But there are two more permanent techniques that have become widely used for identification.

The puppy microchip implantation involves the injection of a small microchip, about the size of a corn kernel, under the skin of the dog. If your dog shows up at a clinic or shelter, or is offered for resale under less than savoury circumstances, it can be positively identified by the microchip. The microchip is scanned, and a registry quickly identifies you as the owner. This is not only protection against theft, but should the dog run away or go chasing a squirrel and become lost, you have a fair chance of his being returned to you.

Tattooing is done on various parts of the dog, from his belly to his cheeks. The number tattooed can be your telephone number or any other number that you can easily memorise. When professional dog thieves see a tattooed dog, they usually lose interest. Both microchipping and tattooing can be done at your local veterinary clinic. For the safety of our dogs, no laboratory facility or dog broker will accept a tattooed dog as stock.

Proper identification tags are a simple way to increase the odds of your Deerhound's being returned to you should he run away.

# Training Your
# DEERHOUND

Living with an untrained dog is a lot like owning a piano that you do not know how to play—it is a nice object to look at but it does not do much more than that to bring you pleasure. Now try taking piano lessons, and suddenly the piano comes alive and brings forth magical sounds and rhythms that set your heart singing and your body swaying.

The same is true with your Deerhound. Any dog is a big responsibility and, if not trained sensibly, may develop unacceptable behaviour that annoys you or could even cause family friction.

To train your Deerhound, you may like to enrol in an obedience class. Teach your dog good manners as you learn how and why he behaves the way he does. Find out how to communicate with your dog and how to recognise and understand his communications with you. Suddenly the dog takes on a new role in your life—he is clever, interesting, well behaved and fun to be with. He demonstrates his bond of devotion to you daily. In other words, your Deerhound does wonders for your ego because he constantly reminds you that you are not only his leader, you are his hero!

Those involved with teaching dog obedience and counselling owners about their dogs' behaviour have discovered some interesting facts about dog ownership. For example, training dogs when they are puppies results in the highest rate of success in developing well-mannered and well-adjusted adult dogs. Training an older dog, from six months to six years of age, can produce almost equal results providing that the owner accepts the dog's slower rate of learning capability and is willing to work patiently to help the dog succeed at developing to his fullest potential. Unfortunately, many owners of untrained adult dogs lack the patience factor, so they do not persist until their dogs are successful at learning particular behaviours.

Training a puppy aged 10 to 16 weeks (20 weeks at the most) is like working with a dry sponge in a pool of water. The pup soaks up whatever you show him and constantly looks for more things to do and learn. At this early age, his body is not yet producing hormones, and therein lies the reason for such a high rate of success. Without hormones, he is focused on his owners and not particularly interested in investigating other places, dogs, people,

**REAP THE REWARDS**

If you start with a normal, healthy dog and give him time, patience and some carefully executed lessons, you will reap the rewards of that training for the life of the dog. And what a life it will be! The two of you will find immeasurable pleasure in the companionship you have built together with love, respect and understanding.

*Keeping the pup's attention is half the battle in training, so it doesn't hurt to enlist some food rewards as motivators.*

etc. You are his leader: his provider of food, water, shelter and security. He latches onto you and wants to stay close. He will usually follow you from room to room, will not let you out of his sight when you are outdoors with him and will respond in like manner to the people and animals you encounter. If you greet a friend warmly, he will be happy to greet the person as well. If, however, you are hesitant or anxious about the approach of a stranger, he will respond accordingly.

Once the puppy begins to produce hormones, his natural curiosity emerges and he begins to investigate the world around him. It is at this time when you may notice that the untrained dog begins to wander away from you and even ignore your commands to stay close. When this behaviour becomes a problem, you have two choices: get rid of the dog or train him. It is strongly urged that you choose the latter option.

You usually will be able to find obedience classes within a reasonable distance from your home, but you can also do a lot to train your dog yourself. Sometimes there are classes available, but the tuition is too costly. Whatever the circumstances, the solution to training your dog without obedience classes lies within the pages of this book.

This chapter is devoted to helping you train your Deerhound at home. If the recommended procedures are followed faithfully, you may expect positive results that will prove rewarding both to

## HONOUR AND OBEY

Dogs are the most honourable animals in existence. They consider another species (humans) as their own. They interface with you. You are their leader. Puppies perceive children to be on their level; their actions around small children are different from their behaviour around their adult masters.

## TRAINING TIP

Dogs will do anything for your attention. If you reward the dog when he is calm and resting, you will develop a well-mannered dog. If, on the other hand, you greet your dog excitedly and encourage him to wrestle with you, the dog will greet you the same way and you will have a hyperactive dog on your hands.

you and your dog.

Whether your new charge is a puppy or a mature adult, the methods of teaching and the techniques we use in training basic behaviours are the same. After all, no dog, whether puppy or adult, likes harsh or inhumane methods. All creatures, however, respond favourably to gentle motivational methods and sincere praise and encouragement. Now let us get started.

### HOUSE-TRAINING

You can train a puppy to relieve himself wherever you choose, but this must be somewhere suitable. You should bear in mind from the outset that when your puppy is old enough to go out in public places, any canine deposits must be removed at once. You will always have to carry with you a small plastic bag or 'poop-scoop.'

Outdoor training includes such surfaces as grass, gravel and cement. Indoor training usually means training your dog to

Your puppy looks up to you for love, care, safety, guidance and discipline.

## MEALTIME

Mealtime should be a peaceful time for your puppy. Do not put his food and water bowls in a high-traffic area in the house. For example, give him his own little corner of the kitchen where he can eat undisturbed and where he will not be underfoot. Do not allow small children or other family members to disturb the pup when he is eating.

newspaper. When deciding on the surface and location that you will want your Deerhound to use, be sure it is going to be permanent. Training your dog to grass and then changing your mind a few months later is extremely difficult for both dog and owner.

Next, choose the command you will use each and every time you want your puppy to void. 'Hurry up' and 'Toilet' are examples of commands commonly used by dog owners. Get in the habit of giving the puppy your chosen relief command before you take him out. That way, when he becomes an adult, you will be able to determine if he wants to go out when you ask him. A confirmation will be signs of interest, wagging his tail, watching you intently, going to the door, etc.

## PUPPY'S NEEDS

Your puppy needs to relieve himself after play periods, after each meal, after he has been sleeping and at any time he indicates that he is looking for a place to urinate or defecate. The urinary and intestinal tract muscles of very young puppies are not fully developed. Therefore, like human babies, puppies need to relieve themselves frequently.

Take your puppy out often—every hour for an eight-week-old, for example—and always immediately after sleeping and eating. The older the puppy, the less often he will need to relieve himself. Finally, as a mature healthy adult, he will require only three to five relief trips per day.

## HOUSING

Since the types of housing and control you provide for your puppy have a direct relationship on the success of house-training, we consider the various aspects of both before we begin training.

Taking a new puppy home and turning him loose in your house can be compared to turning a child loose in a sports arena and telling the child that the place is all his! The sheer enormity of the place would be too much for him to handle. Instead, offer the puppy clearly defined areas where he can play, sleep, eat and live. A room of the house where the

Can you imagine handling a dog as large as a Deerhound—much less two—if it is not properly trained?

family gathers is the most obvious choice. Puppies are social animals and need to feel a part of the pack right from the start. Hearing your voice, watching you while you are doing things and smelling you nearby are all positive reinforcers that he is now a member of your pack. Usually a family room, the

**PAPER CAPER**

Never line your pup's sleeping area with newspaper. Puppy litters are usually raised on newspaper and, once in your home, the puppy will immediately associate newspaper with voiding. Never put newspaper on any floor while house-training, as this will only confuse the puppy. If you are paper-training him, use paper in his designated relief area ONLY. Finally, restrict water intake after evening meals. Offer a few licks at a time—never let a young puppy gulp water after meals.

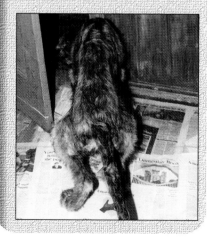

kitchen or a nearby adjoining breakfast area is ideal for providing safety and security for both puppy and owner.

Within the designated room, there should be a smaller area that the puppy can call his own. An alcove, a wire or fibreglass dog crate or a fenced (not boarded!) corner from which he can view the activities of his new family will be fine. The size of the area or crate is the key factor here. The area must be large enough so that the puppy can lie down and stretch out, as well as stand up, without rubbing his head on the top. At the same time, it must be small enough so that he cannot relieve himself at one end and sleep at the other without coming into contact with his droppings before he is fully trained to relieve himself outside. Dogs are, by nature, clean animals and will not remain close to their relief areas unless forced to do so. In those cases, they then become dirty dogs and usually remain that way for life.

The dog's designated area should contain clean bedding and a toy. Water must always be available, in a non-spill container.

**CONTROL**
By control, we mean helping the puppy to create a lifestyle pattern that will be compatible to that of his human pack (YOU!). Just as we guide little children to learn

# CANINE DEVELOPMENT SCHEDULE

It is important to understand how and at what age a puppy develops into adulthood. If you are a puppy owner, consult the following Canine Development Schedule to determine the stage of development your puppy is currently experiencing. This knowledge will help you as you work with the puppy in the weeks and months ahead.

| Period | Age | Characteristics |
|---|---|---|
| FIRST TO THIRD | BIRTH TO SEVEN WEEKS | Puppy needs food, sleep and warmth, and responds to simple and gentle touching. Needs mother for security and disciplining. Needs littermates for learning and interacting with other dogs. Pup learns to function within a pack and learns pack order of dominance. Begin socialising with adults and children for short periods. Begins to become aware of its environment. |
| FOURTH | EIGHT TO TWELVE WEEKS | Brain is fully developed. Needs socialising with outside world. Remove from mother and littermates. Needs to change from canine pack to human pack. Human dominance necessary. Fear period occurs between 8 and 12 weeks. Avoid fright and pain. |
| FIFTH | THIRTEEN TO SIXTEEN WEEKS | Training and formal obedience should begin. Less association with other dogs, more with people, places, situations. Period will pass easily if you remember this is pup's change-to-adolescence time. Be firm and fair. Flight instinct prominent. Permissiveness and over-disciplining can do permanent damage. Praise for good behaviour. |
| JUVENILE | FOUR TO EIGHT MONTHS | Another fear period about 7 to 8 months of age. It passes quickly, but be cautious of fright and pain. Sexual maturity reached. Dominant traits established. Dog should understand sit, down, come and stay by now. |

NOTE: THESE ARE APPROXIMATE TIME FRAMES. ALLOW FOR INDIVIDUAL DIFFERENCES IN PUPPIES.

**KEY TO SUCCESS**
Success that comes by luck is usually short-lived. Success that comes by well-thought-out proven methods is often more easily achieved and permanent. This is the Success Method. It is designed to give you, the puppy owner, a simple yet proven way to help your puppy develop clean living habits and a feeling of security in his new environment.

**HOW MANY TIMES A DAY?**

| AGE | RELIEF TRIPS |
|---|---|
| To 14 weeks | 10 |
| 14–22 weeks | 8 |
| 22–32 weeks | 6 |
| Adulthood | 4 |
| (dog stops growing) | |

These are estimates, of course, but they are a guide to the MINIMUM opportunities a dog should have each day to relieve himself.

our way of life, we must show the puppy when it is time to play, eat, sleep, exercise and even entertain himself.

Your puppy should always sleep in his crate. He should also learn that, during times of household confusion and excessive human activity, such as at breakfast when family members are preparing for the day, he can play by himself in relative safety and comfort in his designated area. Each time you leave the puppy alone, he should understand exactly where he is to stay.

Puppies are chewers. They cannot tell the difference between lamp cords, television wires, shoes, table legs, etc. Chewing into a television wire, for example, can be fatal to the puppy while a shorted wire can start a fire in the house. If the puppy chews on the arm of the chair

when he is alone, you will probably discipline him angrily when you get home. Thus, he makes the association that your coming home means he is going to be punished. (He will not remember chewing the chair and

**THE CLEAN LIFE**
By providing sleeping and resting quarters that fit the dog, and offering frequent opportunities to relieve himself outside his quarters, the puppy quickly learns that the outdoors (or the newspaper if you are training him to paper) is the place to go when he needs to urinate or defecate. It also reinforces his innate desire to keep his sleeping quarters clean. This, in turn, helps develop the muscle control that will eventually produce a dog with clean living habits.

is incapable of making the association of the discipline with his naughty deed.) Accustoming the pup to his designated area not only keeps him safe but also avoids his engaging in destructive behaviours when you are not around.

Times of excitement, such as special occasions, family parties, etc., can be fun for the puppy providing that he can view the activities from the security of his

Always clean up after your Deerhound, whether you are in a public place or in your own garden.

designated area. He is not underfoot and he is not being fed all sorts of titbits that will

# THE SUCCESS METHOD

## *6 Steps to Successful Crate Training*

**1** Tell the puppy 'Crate time!' and place him in the crate with a small treat (a piece of cheese or half of a biscuit). Let him stay in the crate for five minutes while you are in the same room. Then release him and praise lavishly. Never release him when he is fussing. Wait until he is quiet before you let him out.

**2** Repeat Step 1 several times a day.

**3** The next day, place the puppy in the crate as before. Let him stay there for ten minutes. Do this several times.

**4** Continue building time in five-minute increments until the puppy stays in his crate for 30 minutes with you in the room. Always take him to his relief area after prolonged periods in his crate.

**5** Now go back to Step 1 and let the puppy stay in his crate for five minutes, this time while you are out of the room.

**6** Once again, build crate time in five-minute increments with you out of the room. When the puppy will stay willingly in his crate (he may even fall asleep!) for 30 minutes with you out of the room, he will be ready to stay in it for several hours at a time.

probably cause him stomach distress, yet he still feels a part of the fun.

SCHEDULE

A puppy should be taken to his relief area each time he is released from his designated area, after meals, after a play session and when he first awakens in the morning (at age eight weeks, this can mean 5 a.m.!). The puppy will indicate that he's ready 'to go' by circling or sniffing busily—do not misinterpret these signs. For a puppy less than ten weeks of age, a routine of taking him out every hour is necessary. As the puppy grows, he will be able to wait for longer periods of time.

Keep trips to his relief area short. Stay no more than five or six minutes and then return to the

> **'NO' MEANS 'NO!'**
> Dogs do not understand our language. They can be trained to react to a certain sound, at a certain volume. If you say 'No, Oliver' in a very soft pleasant voice, it will not have the same meaning as 'No, Oliver!!' when you shout it as loud as you can. You should never use the dog's name during a reprimand, just the command NO!!

house. If he goes during that time, praise him lavishly and take him indoors immediately. If he does not, but he has an accident when you go back indoors, pick him up immediately, say 'No! No!' and return to his relief area. Wait a few minutes, then return to the house again. Never hit a puppy or

**Dogs respond best to structure. Establishg a toileting schedule with your puppy and do your best to stick to it.**

rub his face in urine or excrement when he has had an accident!

Once indoors, put the puppy in his crate until you have had time to clean up his accident. Then, release him to the family area and watch him more closely than before. Chances are, his accident was a result of your not picking up his signal or waiting too long before offering him the opportunity to relieve himself. Never hold a grudge against the puppy for accidents.

Let the puppy learn that going outdoors means it is time to relieve himself, not to play. Once trained, he will be able to play indoors and out and still differentiate between the times for play versus the times for relief.

Help him develop regular hours for naps, being alone, playing by himself and just resting, all in his crate. Encourage him to entertain himself while you are busy with your activities. Let him learn that having you near is comforting, but it is not your main purpose in life to provide him with undivided attention.

Each time you put your puppy in his own area, use the same command, whatever suits best. Soon he will run to his crate or special area when he hears you say those words.

Crate training provides safety for you, the puppy and the home. It also provides the puppy with a feeling of security, and that helps the puppy achieve self-confidence and clean habits. Remember that one of the primary ingredients in

## TRAINING RULES

If you want to be successful in training your dog, you have four rules to obey yourself:
1. Develop an understanding of how a dog thinks.
2. Do not blame the dog for lack of communication.
3. Define your dog's personality and act accordingly.
4. Have patience and be consistent.

house-training your puppy is control. Regardless of your lifestyle, there will always be occasions when you will need to have a place where your dog can stay and be happy and safe.

In conclusion, a few key elements are really all you need for a successful house-training method—consistency, frequency, praise, control and supervision.

### PLAN TO PLAY

The puppy should also have regular play and exercise sessions when he is with you or a family member. Exercise for a very young puppy can consist of a short walk around the house or garden. Playing can include fetching games with a large ball or a special raggy. (All puppies teethe and need soft things upon which to chew.) Remember to restrict play periods to indoors within his living area (the family room, for example) until he is completely house-trained.

By following these procedures with a normal, healthy puppy, you and the puppy will soon be past the stage of 'accidents' and ready to move on to a full and rewarding life together.

### ROLES OF DISCIPLINE, REWARD AND PUNISHMENT

Discipline, training one to act in accordance with rules, brings order to life. It is as simple as that. Without discipline, particularly in a group society, chaos will reign supreme and the group will eventually perish. Humans and canines are social animals and need some form of discipline in order to function effectively. They must procure food, protect their home base and their young and reproduce to keep their species going. If there were no discipline in the lives of social animals, they would eventually die from starvation and/or predation by other stronger animals.

In the case of domestic canines, discipline in their lives is needed in order for them to understand how their pack (you and other family members) functions and how they must act in order to survive.

A large humane society in a highly populated area recently surveyed dog owners regarding their satisfaction with their relationships with their dogs. People who had trained their dogs were 75% more satisfied with

## KEEP SMILING

Never train your dog, puppy or adult, when you are angry or in a sour mood. Dogs are very sensitive to human feelings, especially anger, and if your dog senses that you are angry or upset, he will connect your anger with his training and learn to resent or fear his training sessions.

their pets than those who had never trained their dogs.

Dr Edward Thorndike, a psychologist, established *Thorndike's Theory of Learning*, which states that a behaviour that results in a pleasant event tends to be repeated. A behaviour that results in an unpleasant event tends not to be repeated. It is this theory upon which training methods are based today. For example, if you manipulate a dog to perform a specific behaviour and reward him for doing it, he is likely to do it again because he enjoyed the end result.

Occasionally, punishment, a penalty inflicted for an offence, is necessary. The best type of punishment often comes from an outside source. For example, a child is told not to touch the stove because he may get burned. He disobeys and touches the stove. In doing so, he receives a burn. From that time on, he respects the heat of the stove and avoids contact with it. Therefore, a behaviour

that results in an unpleasant event tends not to be repeated.

A good example of a dog learning the hard way is the dog who chases the house cat. He is told many times to leave the cat alone, yet he persists in teasing the cat. Then, one day, the dog begins chasing the cat but the cat turns and swipes a claw across the dog's face, leaving the dog with a painful gash on his nose. The final result is that the dog stops chasing the cat. Again, a behaviour that results in an unpleasant event tends not to be repeated.

All training should take place with your Deerhound on lead. Only attempt off-lead training in a securely fenced area.

## TRAINING EQUIPMENT

### COLLAR AND LEAD
For a Deerhound, the collar and lead that you use for training must be one with which you are easily able to work, not too heavy for the dog and perfectly safe.

### TREATS
Have a bag of treats on hand; something nutritious and easy to swallow works best. Use a soft treat, a chunk of cheese or a piece of cooked chicken rather than a dry biscuit. By the time the dog has finished chewing a dry treat, he will forget why he is being rewarded in the first place!

Using food rewards will not teach a dog to beg at the table—the only way to teach a dog to beg at the table is to give him food from the table. In training, rewarding the dog with a food treat will help him associate praise and the treats with learning new behaviours that obviously please his owner.

## TRAINING BEGINS: ASK THE DOG A QUESTION
In order to teach your dog anything, you must first get his attention. After all, he cannot learn anything if he is looking away from you with his mind on something else.

To get your dog's attention, ask him 'School?' and immediately walk over to him and give him a treat as you tell him 'Good dog.' Wait a minute or two and repeat the routine, this time with a treat in your hand as you approach within a foot of the dog. Do not go directly to him, but stop about a foot short of him and hold out the treat as you ask 'School?' He will see you approaching with a treat in your hand and most likely begin walking toward you. As you meet, give him the treat and praise again.

The third time, ask the question, have a treat in your hand and walk only a short distance toward the dog so that he must walk almost all the way to you. As he reaches you, give him the treat and praise again.

By this time, the dog will probably be getting the idea that if he pays attention to you, especially when you ask that question, it will pay off in treats and enjoyable activities for him. In other words, he learns that 'school' means doing great things with you that are fun and that result in positive attention for him.

Remember that the dog does not understand your verbal language; he only recognises sounds. Your question translates to a series of sounds for him, and those sounds become the signal to go to you and pay attention. The dog learns that if he does this, he will get to interact with you plus receive treats and praise.

such as 'Good dog! Good sit!,' etc. Remember to always praise enthusiastically, because dogs relish verbal praise from their owners and feel so proud of themselves whenever they accomplish a behaviour.

You will not use food forever in getting the dog to obey your commands. Food is only used to teach new behaviours and, once the dog knows what you want when you give a specific command, you will wean him off the food treats but still maintain the verbal praise. After all, you will always have your voice with you, and there will be many times when you have no food rewards but expect the dog to obey.

In teaching the sit exercise, you may have to begin by guiding your dog into the sit position until he gets the idea.

## THE BASIC COMMANDS

### TEACHING SIT

Now that you have the dog's attention, attach his lead and hold it in your left hand, and hold a food treat in your right hand. Place your food hand at the dog's nose and let him lick the treat but not take it from you. Say 'Sit' and slowly raise your food hand from in front of the dog's nose up over his head so that he is looking at the ceiling. As he bends his head upward, he will have to bend his knees to maintain his balance. As he bends his knees, he will assume a sit position. At that point, release the food treat and praise lavishly with comments

Once the sit command is learned, practise it at the beginning and end of every lesson. Success builds confidence in the Deerhound pupil.

### TEACHING DOWN

Teaching the down exercise is easy when you understand how the dog perceives the down position, and it is very difficult when you do not. Dogs perceive the down position as a submissive one; therefore, teaching the down exercise by using a forceful method can sometimes make the dog develop such a fear of the down that he either runs away when you say 'Down' or he attempts to snap at the person who tries to force him down.

Have the dog sit close alongside your left leg, facing in the same direction as you are. Hold the lead in your left hand and a food treat in your right. Now place your left hand lightly on the top of the dog's shoulders where they meet above the spinal cord. Do not push down on the dog's shoulders; simply rest your left hand there so you can guide the dog to lie down close to your left leg rather than to swing away from your side when he drops.

Now place the food hand at the dog's nose, say 'Down' very softly (almost a whisper), and slowly lower the food hand to the dog's front feet. When the food hand reaches the floor, begin moving it forward along the floor in front of the dog. Keep talking softly to the dog, saying things like, 'Do you want this treat? You can do this, good dog.' Your reassuring tone of voice will help calm the dog as he tries to follow the food hand in order to get the treat.

When the dog's elbows touch the floor, release the food and praise softly. Try to get the dog to maintain that down position for several seconds before you let him sit up again. The goal here is to get the dog to settle down and not feel threatened in the down position.

### DOUBLE JEOPARDY

A dog in jeopardy never lies down. He stays alert on his feet because instinct tells him that he may have to run away or fight for his survival. Therefore, if a dog feels threatened or anxious, he will not lie down. Consequently, it is important to have the dog calm and relaxed as he learns the down exercise.

## CONSISTENCY PAYS OFF

Dogs need consistency in their feeding schedule, exercise and toilet breaks, and in the verbal commands you use. If you use 'Stay' on Monday and 'Stay here, please' on Tuesday, you will confuse your dog. Don't demand perfect behaviour during training classes and then let him have the run of the house the rest of the day. Above all, lavish praise on your pet consistently every time he does something right. The more he feels he is pleasing you, the more willing he will be to learn.

### TEACHING STAY

It is easy to teach the dog to stay in either a sit or a down position. Again, we use food and praise during the teaching process as we help the dog to understand exactly what it is that we are expecting him to do.

To teach the sit/stay, start with the dog sitting on your left side as before and hold the lead in your left hand. Have a food treat in your right hand and place your food hand at the dog's nose. Say 'Stay' and step out on your right foot to stand directly in front of the dog, toe to toe, as he licks and nibbles the treat. Be sure to keep his head facing upward to maintain the sit position. Count to five and then swing around to stand next to the dog again with him on your left. As soon as you

get back to the original position, release the food and praise lavishly.

To teach the down/stay, do the down as previously described. As soon as the dog lies down, say 'Stay' and step out on your right foot just as you did in the sit/stay. Count to five and then return to stand beside the dog with him on your left side. Release the treat and praise as always.

Within a week or ten days, you can begin to add a bit of distance between you and your dog when you leave him. When you do, use your left hand open with the palm facing the dog as a stay signal, much the same as the hand signal a constable uses to stop traffic at an intersection. Hold the food treat in your right hand as before, but this time the food will not be touching the

Young puppies naturally stay close to their owners and will follow them from place to place, but puppies grow curious and tend to explore, which is why teaching the dog to come to you is so important.

**'WHERE ARE YOU?'**
When calling the dog, do not say 'Come.' Say things like, 'Rover, where are you? See if you can find me! I have a biscuit for you!' Keep up a constant line of chatter with coaxing sounds and frequent questions such as, 'Where are you?' The dog will learn to follow the sound of your voice to locate you and receive his reward.

### TEACHING COME

If you make teaching 'come' an exciting experience, you should never have a 'student' that does not love the game or that fails to come when called. The secret, it seems, is never to teach the word 'come.'

At times when an owner most wants his dog to come when called, the owner is likely to be upset or anxious and he allows these feelings to come through in the tone of his voice when he calls his dog. Hearing that desperation in his owner's voice, the dog fears the results of going to him and therefore either disobeys outright or runs in the opposite direction. The secret, therefore, is to teach the dog a game and, when you want him to come to you, simply play the game. It is practically a no-fail solution!

To begin, have several members of your family take a few food treats and each go into a different room in the house.

dog's nose. He will watch the food hand and quickly learn that he is going to get that treat as soon as you return to his side.

When you can stand 1 metre away from your dog for 30 seconds, you can then begin building time and distance in both stays. Eventually, the dog can be expected to remain in the stay position for prolonged periods of time until you return to him or call him to you. Always praise lavishly when he stays.

**'COME' . . . BACK**
Never call your dog to come to you for a correction or scold him when he reaches you. That is the quickest way to turn a 'Come' command into 'Go away fast!' Dogs think only in the present tense, and your dog will connect the scolding with coming to you, not with the misbehaviour of a few moments earlier.

Everyone takes turns calling the dog, and each person should celebrate the dog's finding him with a treat and lots of happy praise. When a person calls the dog, he is actually inviting the dog to find him and to get a treat as a reward for 'winning.'

A few turns of the 'Where are you?' game and the dog will understand that everyone is playing the game and that each person has a big celebration awaiting the dog's success at locating him or her. Once the dog learns to love the game, simply calling out 'Where are you?' will bring him running from wherever he is when he hears that all-important question.

The come command is recognised as one of the most important things to teach a dog, but there are trainers who work with thousands of dogs and never teach the actual word 'come.' Yet these dogs will race to respond to a person who uses the dog's name followed by 'Where are you?' For example, a woman has a 10-year-old companion dog who went blind, but who never fails to locate her owner when asked, 'Where are you?'

Children, in particular, love to play this game with their dogs. Children can hide in smaller places like a shower or bath, behind a bed or under a table. The dog needs to work a little bit harder to find these hiding

## FEAR AGGRESSION

Pups who are subjected to physical abuse during training commonly end up with behavioural problems as adults. One common result of abuse is fear aggression, in which a dog will lash out, bare his teeth, snarl and finally bite someone by whom he feels threatened. For example, your daughter may be playing with the dog one afternoon. As they play hide-and-seek, she backs the dog into a corner and, as she attempts to tease him playfully, he bites her hand. Examine the cause of this behaviour. Did your daughter ever hit the dog? Did someone who resembles your daughter hit or scream at the dog?

Fortunately, fear aggression is relatively easy to correct. Have your daughter engage in only positive activities with the dog, such as feeding, petting and walking. She should not give any corrections or negative feedback. If the dog still growls or cowers away from her, allow someone else to accompany them. After approximately one week, the dog should feel that he can rely on her for many positive things, and he will also be prevented from reacting fearfully towards anyone who might resemble her.

places, but, when he does, he loves to celebrate with a treat and a tussle with a favourite youngster.

owner) will not proceed unless the dog is walking calmly beside him. Neither pulling out ahead on the lead nor lagging behind is acceptable.

Begin by holding the lead in your left hand as the dog sits beside your left leg. Move the loop end of the lead to your right hand, but keep your left hand short on the lead so that it keeps the dog in close next to you.

Say 'Heel' and step forward on your left foot. Keep the dog close to you and take three steps. Stop and have the dog sit next to you in what we now call the 'heel position.' Praise verbally, but do not touch the dog. Hesitate a moment and begin again with 'Heel,' taking three steps and stopping, at which point the dog is told to sit again.

Your goal here is to have the dog walk those three steps without pulling on the lead. Once he will walk calmly beside you for three steps without pulling, increase the number of steps you take to five. When he will walk politely beside you while you take

### TUG OF WALK?

If you begin teaching the heel by taking long walks and letting the dog pull you along, he misinterprets this action as an acceptable form of taking a walk. When you pull back on the lead to counteract his pulling, he reads that tug as a signal to pull even harder!

### TEACHING HEEL

Heeling means that the dog walks beside the owner without pulling. It takes time and patience on the owner's part to succeed at teaching the dog that he (the

### HEELING WELL

Teach your dog to heel in an enclosed area. Once you think the dog will obey reliably and you want to attempt advanced obedience exercises such as off-lead heeling, test him in a fenced-in area so he cannot run away.

five steps, you can increase the length of your walk to ten steps. Keep increasing the length of your stroll until the dog will walk quietly beside you without pulling as long as you want him to heel. When you stop heeling, indicate to the dog that the exercise is over by verbally praising as you pet him and say 'OK, good dog.' The 'OK' is used as a release word, meaning that the exercise is finished and the dog is free to relax.

If you are dealing with a dog who insists on pulling you around, simply 'put on your brakes' and stand your ground until the dog realises that the two of you are not going anywhere until he is beside you and moving at your pace, not his. It may take some time just standing there to convince the dog that you are the leader and that you will be the one to decide on the direction and speed of your travel.

Each time the dog looks up at you or slows down to give a slack lead between the two of you, quietly praise him and say, 'Good heel. Good dog.' Eventually, the dog will begin to respond and within a few days he will be walking politely beside you without pulling on the lead. At first, the training sessions should be kept short and very positive; soon the dog will be able to walk nicely with you for increasingly longer distances. Remember also to give the dog free time and the opportunity to run and play when you have finished heel practice.

This four-month-old puppy is practising the heel exercise at a swift pace.

## OBEDIENCE CLASSES

It is a good idea to enrol in an obedience class if one is available in your area. If yours is a show dog, ringcraft classes would be more appropriate. Many areas have dog clubs that offer basic obedience training as well as preparatory classes for obedience competition. There are also local dog trainers who offer similar classes.

At obedience shows, dogs can earn titles at various levels of competition. The beginning levels of obedience competition include basic behaviours such as sit, down, heel, etc. The more advanced levels of competition include jumping, retrieving, scent discrimination and signal work. The advanced levels require a dog and owner to put a lot of time and effort into their training. The titles that can be earned at these levels of competition are very prestigious.

## OTHER ACTIVITIES FOR LIFE

Whether a dog is trained in the structured environment of a class or alone with his owner at home, there are many activities that can bring fun and rewards to both owner and dog once they have mastered basic control.

Teaching the dog to help out around the home, in the garden or on the farm provides great satisfaction to both dog and owner. In addition, the dog's help makes life a little easier for his owner and raises the dog's stature as a valued companion to his family. It helps give the dog a purpose by occupying his mind and providing an outlet for his energy.

### HOW TO WEAN THE 'TREAT HOG'

If you have trained your dog by rewarding him with a treat each time he performs a command, he may soon decide that without the treat, he won't sit, stay or come. The best way to fix this problem is to start asking your dog to do certain commands twice before being rewarded. Slowly increase the number of commands given and then vary the number: three sits and a treat one day, five sits for a biscuit the next day, etc. Your dog will soon realise that there is no set number of sits before he gets his reward, and he'll likely do it the first time you ask in the hope of being rewarded sooner rather than later.

If you are interested in participating in organised competition with your Deerhound, there are activities other than obedience in which you and your dog can become involved.

## AGILITY TRIALS

Although not a sport in which many Deerhounds participate, agility is a popular sport in which dogs run through an obstacle course that includes various jumps, tunnels and other exercises to test the dog's speed and co-ordination. The owners run beside their dogs to give commands and to guide them through the course. Although competitive, the focus is on fun— it's fun to do, fun to watch and great exercise.

## COURSING AND LURE COURSING

Many Deerhounds and their owners enjoy the sport of hare coursing. This is a way in which enthusiasts endeavour to maintain the breed's working qualities, even though the original work of the Deerhound no longer exists. Hare coursing for Deerhounds is organised under National Coursing Club and Deerhound Club rules.

It is well known that coursing is opposed by many; however, one should realise that the purpose is to compare dogs' speed and agility, rather than to catch the hare. Indeed a high percentage of courses do not end in a kill, and, contrary to belief, hares are certainly not released from boxes without a means of escape.

In lure coursing, the dogs chase a lure, which, of course, cannot change direction, as can live quarry. The coursing takes place between spring and autumn; it is great fun and has less pressure than more competitive events.

If you hope to show your Deerhound, ringcraft classes and practice at home will help to prepare both of you for the ring.

A Deerhound in full flight in a coursing event is spectacular to watch.

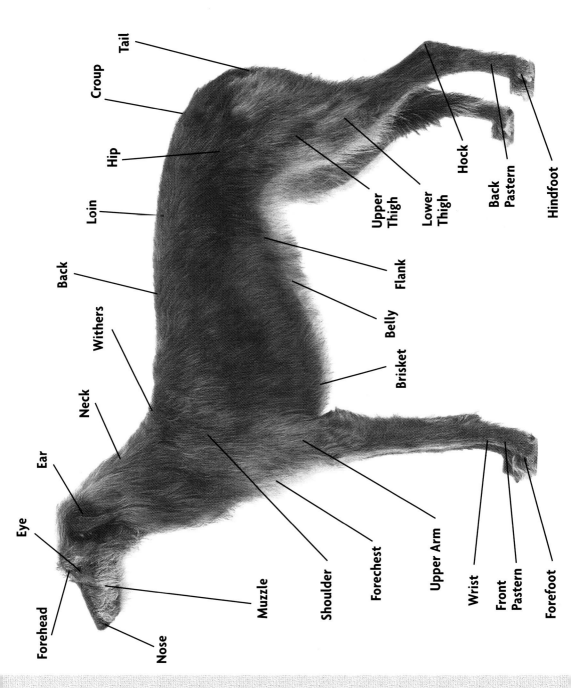

Tail

Croup

Hip

Loin

Back

Withers

Neck

Ear

Eye

Forehead

Nose

Muzzle

Shoulder

Forechest

Upper Arm

Wrist

Front Pastern

Forefoot

Brisket

Belly

Flank

Upper Thigh

Lower Thigh

Hock

Back Pastern

Hindfoot

PHYSICAL STRUCTURE OF THE DEERHOUND

# Health Care of Your
# DEERHOUND

Dogs suffer from many of the same physical illnesses as people. They might even share many of the same psychological problems. Since people usually know more about human diseases than canine maladies, many of the terms used in this chapter will be familiar but not necessarily those used by veterinary surgeons. We will use the term *x-ray*, instead of the more acceptable term *radiograph*. We will also use the familiar term *symptoms* even though dogs don't have symptoms, which are verbal descriptions of the patient's feelings; dogs have *clinical signs*. Since dogs can't speak, we have to look for clinical signs...but we still use the term *symptoms* in this book.

As a general rule, medicine is *practised*. That term is not arbitrary. Medicine is a constantly changing art as we learn more and more about genetics, electronic aids (like CAT scans) and daily laboratory advances. There are many dog maladies, like canine hip dysplasia, which are not universally treated in the same manner. Some veterinary surgeons opt for surgery more often than others do.

## SELECTING A VETERINARY SURGEON

Your selection of a veterinary surgeon should not be based upon personality (as most are) but upon his convenience to your home. You want a vet who is close because you might have emergencies or need to make multiple visits for treatments. You want a vet who has services that you might require such as tattooing and grooming, as well as sophisticated pet supplies and a good reputation for ability and responsiveness. There is nothing more frustrating than having to wait a day or more to get a response from a veterinary surgeon.

All veterinary surgeons are licensed and their diplomas and/or certificates should be displayed in their waiting rooms. There are, however, many veterinary specialities that usually require further studies and internships. There are specialists in heart problems (veterinary cardiologists), skin problems (veterinary dermatologists), teeth and gum problems (veterinary dentists), eye problems (veterinary ophthalmologists) and x-rays (veterinary radiologists), as well as vets who have

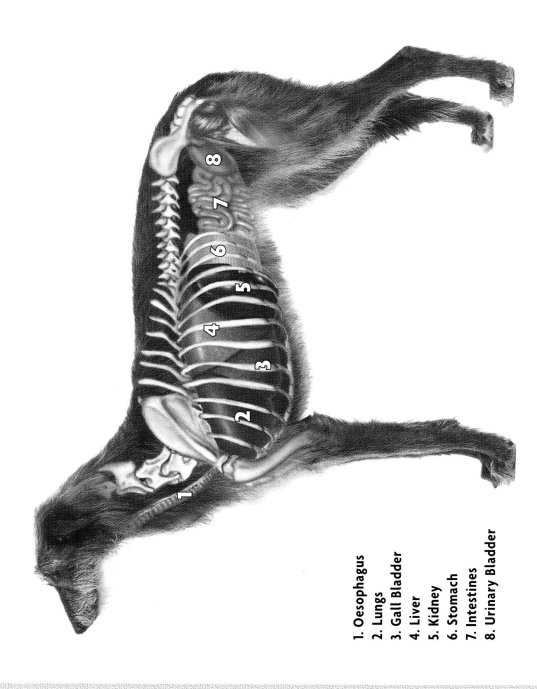

1. Oesophagus
2. Lungs
3. Gall Bladder
4. Liver
5. Kidney
6. Stomach
7. Intestines
8. Urinary Bladder

# INTERNAL ORGANS OF THE DEERHOUND

specialities in bones, muscles or other organs. Most veterinary surgeons do routine surgery such as neutering, stitching up wounds and docking tails for those breeds in which such is required for show purposes.

When the problem affecting your dog is serious, it is not unusual or impudent to get another medical opinion, although in Britain you are obliged to advise the vets concerned about this. You might also want to compare costs among several veterinary surgeons. Sophisticated health care and veterinary services can be very costly. It is not infrequent that important decisions are based upon financial considerations.

## PREVENTATIVE MEDICINE

It is much easier, less costly and more effective to practise preventative medicine than to fight bouts of illness and disease. Properly bred puppies come from parents who were selected based upon their genetic disease profiles. Their mothers should have been vaccinated, free of all internal and external parasites and properly nourished. The dam can pass on disease resistance to her puppies, which can last for eight to ten weeks, but she can also pass on parasites and many infections. For these reasons, a visit to the veterinary surgeon who cared for the dam is recommended.

VACCINATION SCHEDULING
Most vaccinations are given by injection and should only be done by a veterinary surgeon. Both he and you should keep records of the date of the injection, the identification of the vaccine and the amount given. Some vets give a first vaccination at eight weeks, but most dog breeders prefer the course not to commence until about ten weeks to avoid negating any antibodies passed on by the dam. The vaccination scheduling is usually based on a 15-day cycle. You must take your vet's advice regarding when to vaccinate, as this may differ according to the vaccine used. Most vaccinations immunize your puppy against viruses.

The usual vaccines contain immunizing doses of several different viruses such as distemper, parvovirus, parainfluenza and hepatitis, although some veterinary surgeons recommend separate vaccines for each disease. There are other vaccines available when the puppy is at risk. You should rely upon professional advice. This is especially true for the booster-shot programme. Most vaccination programmes require a booster when the puppy is a year old and once a year thereafter. In some cases, circumstances may require more or less frequent immunizations. Kennel cough, more formally known as tracheobronchitis, is treated with a vaccine that is

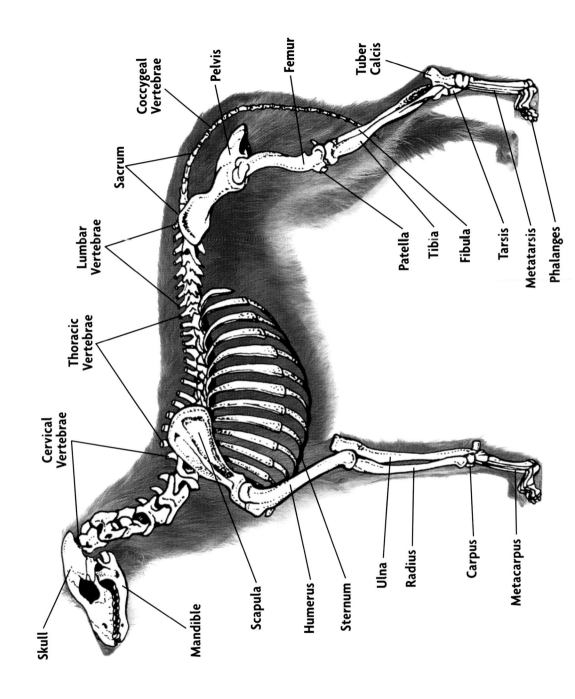

SKELETAL STRUCTURE OF THE DEERHOUND

Coccygeal Vertebrae

Pelvis

Femur

Tuber Calcis

Sacrum

Lumbar Vertebrae

Thoracic Vertebrae

Cervical Vertebrae

Patella

Tibia

Fibula

Tarsis

Metatarsis

Phalanges

Skull

Mandible

Scapula

Humerus

Sternum

Ulna

Radius

Carpus

Metacarpus

sprayed into the dog's nostrils. Kennel cough is usually included in routine vaccination, but this is often not so effective as for other major diseases.

### WEANING TO FIVE MONTHS OLD

Puppies should be weaned by the time they are about two months old. A puppy that remains for at least eight weeks with its mother and littermates usually adapts better to other dogs and people later in life. Some new owners have their puppies examined by veterinary surgeons immediately, which is a good idea. Vaccination programmes usually begin when the puppy is very young.

The puppy will have its teeth examined, and have its skeletal conformation and general health checked prior to certification by the veterinary surgeon. Puppies in certain breeds may have problems with their kneecaps, cataracts and other eye problems, heart murmurs or undescended testicles. They may also have personality problems, and your veterinary surgeon might have training in temperament evaluation.

### FIVE TO TWELVE MONTHS OF AGE

Unless you intend to breed or show your dog, neutering the puppy at six months of age is recommended. Discuss this with your veterinary

# HEALTH AND VACCINATION SCHEDULE

| AGE IN WEEKS: | 6TH | 8TH | 10TH | 12TH | 14TH | 16TH | 20-24TH | 1 YR |
|---|---|---|---|---|---|---|---|---|
| Worm Control | ✔ | ✔ | ✔ | ✔ | ✔ | ✔ | ✔ | |
| Neutering | | | | | | | | ✔ |
| Heartworm | | ✔ | | ✔ | | ✔ | ✔ | |
| Parvovirus | ✔ | | ✔ | | ✔ | | ✔ | ✔ |
| Distemper | | ✔ | | ✔ | | ✔ | | ✔ |
| Hepatitis | | ✔ | | ✔ | | ✔ | | ✔ |
| Leptospirosis | | | | | | | | ✔ |
| Parainfluenza | ✔ | | ✔ | | ✔ | | | ✔ |
| Dental Examination | | ✔ | | | | | ✔ | ✔ |
| Complete Physical | | ✔ | | | | | ✔ | ✔ |
| Coronavirus | | | | ✔ | | | ✔ | ✔ |
| Kennel Cough | ✔ | | | | | | | |
| Hip Dysplasia | | | | | | | | ✔ |
| Rabies | | | | | | | ✔ | |

Vaccinations are not instantly effective. It takes about two weeks for the dog's immune system to develop antibodies. Most vaccinations require annual booster shots. Your veterinary surgeon should guide you in this regard.

surgeon. Neutering has proved to be extremely beneficial to both male and female puppies. Besides eliminating the possibility of pregnancy, it inhibits (but does not prevent) breast cancer in bitches and prostate cancer in male dogs. Under no circumstances should a bitch be spayed prior to her first season.

Your veterinary surgeon should provide your puppy with a thorough dental evaluation at six months of age, ascertaining whether all the permanent teeth have erupted properly. A home dental care regimen should be initiated at six months, including brushing weekly and providing good dental devices (such as nylon bones). Regular dental care promotes healthy teeth, fresh breath and a longer life.

### ONE TO SEVEN YEARS

Once a year, your grown dog should visit the vet for an examination and vaccination boosters, if needed. Some vets recommend blood tests, a thyroid level check and a dental evaluation to accompany these annual visits. A

# DISEASE REFERENCE CHART

| | What is it? | What causes it? | Symptoms |
|---|---|---|---|
| **Leptospirosis** | Severe disease that affects the internal organs; can be spread to people. | A bacterium, which is often carried by rodents, that enters through mucous membranes and spreads quickly throughout the body. | Range from fever, vomiting and loss of appetite in less severe cases to shock, irreversible kidney damage and possibly death in most severe cases. |
| **Rabies** | Potentially deadly virus that infects warm-blooded mammals. Not seen in United Kingdom. | Bite from a carrier of the virus, mainly wild animals. | 1st stage: dog exhibits change in behaviour, fear. 2nd stage: dog's behaviour becomes more aggressive. 3rd stage: loss of coordination, trouble with bodily functions. |
| **Parvovirus** | Highly contagious virus, potentially deadly. | Ingestion of the virus, which is usually spread through the faeces of infected dogs. | Most common: severe diarrhoea. Also vomiting, fatigue, lack of appetite. |
| **Kennel cough** | Contagious respiratory infection. | Combination of types of bacteria and virus. Most common: *Bordetella bronchiseptica* bacteria and parainfluenza virus. | Chronic cough. |
| **Distemper** | Disease primarily affecting respiratory and nervous system. | Virus that is related to the human measles virus. | Mild symptoms such as fever, lack of appetite and mucous secretion progress to evidence of brain damage, 'hard pad.' |
| **Hepatitis** | Virus primarily affecting the liver. | Canine adenovirus type I (CAV-1). Enters system when dog breathes in particles. | Lesser symptoms include listlessness, diarrhoea, vomiting. More severe symptoms include 'blue-eye' (clumps of virus in eye). |
| **Coronavirus** | Virus resulting in digestive problems. | Virus is spread through infected dog's faeces. | Stomach upset evidenced by lack of appetite, vomiting, diarrhoea. |

thorough clinical evaluation by the vet can provide critical background information for your dog. Blood tests are often performed at one year of age, and dental examinations around the third or fourth birthday. In the long run, quality preventative care for your pet can save money, teeth and lives.

## SKIN PROBLEMS

Veterinary surgeons are consulted by dog owners for skin problems more than for any other group of diseases or maladies. Dogs' skin is almost as sensitive as human skin, and both suffer from almost the same ailments (though the occurrence of acne in dogs is rare!). For this reason, veterinary dermatology has developed into a speciality practised by many veterinary surgeons.

Since many skin problems have visual symptoms that are almost identical, it requires the skill of an experienced veterinary dermatologist to identify and cure many of the more severe skin disorders. Pet shops sell many treatments for skin problems, but most of the treatments are directed at the symptoms and not the underlying problem(s). If your dog is suffering from a skin disorder, you should seek professional assistance as quickly as possible. As with all diseases, the earlier a problem is identified and treated, the more successful is the cure.

### HEREDITARY SKIN DISORDERS

Veterinary dermatologists are currently researching a number of skin disorders that is believed to have an hereditary basis. These inherited diseases are transmitted by both parents, who appear (phenotypically) normal but have a recessive gene for the disease, meaning that they carry, but are not affected by, the disease. These diseases pose serious problems to breeders because in some instances there are no methods of identifying carriers. Often the secondary diseases associated with these skin conditions are even more debilitating than the skin disorders themselves, including cancers and respiratory problems; others can be lethal.

Among the hereditary skin disorders, for which the mode of inheritance is known, are: acrodermatitis, cutaneous asthenia (Ehlers-Danlos syndrome), sebaceous adenitis, cyclic hematopoiesis, dermatomyositis, IgA deficiency, colour dilution alopaecia and nodular dermatofibrosis. Some of these disorders are limited to one or two breeds, while others affect a large number of breeds. All inherited diseases must be diagnosed and treated by a veterinary specialist.

### PARASITE BITES

Many of us are allergic to insect bites. The bites itch, erupt and may even become infected. Dogs have

# DO YOU KNOW ABOUT HIP DYSPLASIA?

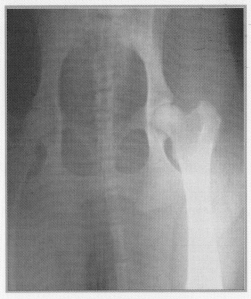

X-ray of a dog with 'Good' hips.

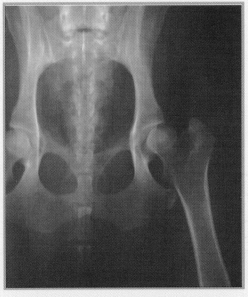

X-ray of a dog with 'Moderate' dysplastic hips.

Hip dysplasia is a fairly common condition found in pure-bred dogs. When a dog has hip dysplasia, its hind leg has an incorrectly formed hip joint. By constant use of the hip joint, it becomes more and more loose, wears abnormally and may become arthritic.

Hip dysplasia can only be confirmed with an x-ray, but certain symptoms may indicate a problem. Your dog may have a hip dysplasia problem if it walks in a peculiar manner, hops instead of smoothly runs, uses its hind legs in unison (to keep the pressure off the weak joint), has trouble getting up from a prone position or always sits with both legs together on one side of its body.

As the dog matures, it may adapt well to life with a bad hip, but in a few years the arthritis develops and many dogs with hip dysplasia become cripples.

Hip dysplasia is considered an inherited disease and only can be diagnosed definitively when the dog is two years old. Some experts claim that a special diet might help your puppy outgrow the bad hip, but the usual treatments are surgical. The removal of the pectineus muscle, the removal of the round part of the femur, reconstructing the pelvis and replacing the hip with an artificial one are all surgical interventions that are expensive, but they are usually very successful. Follow the advice of your veterinary surgeon.

the same reaction to fleas, ticks and/or mites. When an insect lands on you, you have the chance to whisk it away with your hand. Unfortunately, when your dog is bitten by a flea, tick or mite, he can only scratch it away or bite it. By the time the dog has been bitten, the parasite has done some of its damage. It may also have laid eggs, which will cause further problems in the near future. The itching from parasite bites is probably due to the saliva injected into the site when the parasite sucks the dog's blood.

### Auto-Immune Skin Conditions

An auto-immune skin condition is commonly referred to as a condition in which a person (or dog) is 'allergic' to him- or herself, while an allergy is usually an inflammatory reaction to an outside stimulus. Auto-immune diseases cause serious damage to the tissues that are involved.

The best known auto-immune disease is lupus, which affects people as well as dogs. The symptoms are variable and may affect the kidneys, bones, blood chemistry and skin. It can be fatal to both dogs and humans, though it is not thought to be transmissible. It is usually successfully treated with cortisone, prednisone or a similar corticosteroid, but extensive use of these drugs can have harmful side effects.

### Acral Lick Granuloma

Many large dogs have a very poorly understood syndrome called acral lick granuloma. The manifestation of the problem is the dog's tireless attack at a specific area of the body, usually the legs or paws. The dog licks so intensively that he removes the hair and skin, leaving an ugly, large wound. Tiny protuberances, which are outgrowths of new capillaries, bead on the surface of the wound. Owners who notice their dogs' biting and chewing at their extremities should have the vet determine the cause. If lick granuloma is identified, although there is no absolute cure, corticosteroids are one common treatment.

### Airborne Allergies

An annoying allergy is pollen allergy. Humans have hay fever, rose fever and other fevers from which they suffer during the pollinating season. Many dogs suffer the same allergies. When the pollen count is high, your dog might suffer, but don't expect him to sneeze and have a runny nose like a human would. Dogs react to pollen allergies the same way they react to fleas— they scratch and bite themselves.

Dogs, like humans, can be tested for allergens. Discuss the testing with your veterinary surgeon or dermatologist.

# Number-One Killer Disease in Dogs: CANCER

In every age there is a word associated with a disease or plague that causes humans to shudder. In the 21st century, that word is 'cancer.' Just as cancer is the leading cause of death in humans, it claims nearly half the lives of dogs that die from a natural disease as well as half the dogs that die over the age of ten years.

Described as a genetic disease, cancer becomes a greater risk as the dog ages. Veterinary surgeons and dog owners have become increasingly aware of the threat of cancer to dogs. Statistics reveal that one dog in every five will develop cancer, the most common of which is skin cancer. Many cancers, including prostate, ovarian and breast cancer, can be avoided by spaying and neutering our dogs by the age of six months.

Early detection of cancer can save or extend your dog's life, so it is absolutely vital for owners to have their dogs examined by a qualified veterinary surgeon or oncologist immediately upon detection of any abnormality. Certain dietary guidelines have also proven to reduce the onset and spread of cancer. Foods based on fish rather than beef, due to the presence of Omega-3 fatty acids, are recommended. Other amino acids such as glutamine have significant benefits for canines, particularly those breeds that show a greater susceptibility to cancer.

Cancer management and treatments promise hope for future generations of canines. Since the disease is genetic, breeders should never breed a dog whose parents, grandparents and any related siblings have developed cancer. It is difficult to know whether to exclude an otherwise healthy dog from a breeding programme as the disease does not manifest itself until the dog's senior years.

## RECOGNISE CANCER WARNING SIGNS

Since early detection can possibly rescue your dog from becoming a cancer statistic, it is essential for owners to recognise the possible signs and seek the assistance of a qualified professional.

- Abnormal bumps or lumps that continue to grow
- Bleeding or discharge from any body cavity
- Persistent stiffness or lameness
- Recurrent sores or sores that do not heal
- Inappetence
- Breathing difficulties
- Weight loss
- Bad breath or odours
- General malaise and fatigue
- Eating and swallowing problems
- Difficulty urinating and defecating

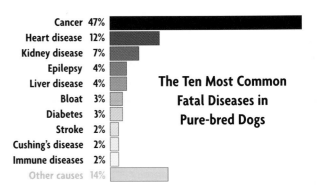

| Disease | Percentage |
|---|---|
| Cancer | 47% |
| Heart disease | 12% |
| Kidney disease | 7% |
| Epilepsy | 4% |
| Liver disease | 4% |
| Bloat | 3% |
| Diabetes | 3% |
| Stroke | 2% |
| Cushing's disease | 2% |
| Immune diseases | 2% |
| Other causes | 14% |

**The Ten Most Common Fatal Diseases in Pure-bred Dogs**

# FOOD PROBLEMS

### FOOD ALLERGIES

Dogs are allergic to many foods that are best-sellers and highly recommended by breeders and veterinary surgeons. Changing the brand of food that you buy may not eliminate the problem if the element to which the dog is allergic is contained in the new brand.

Recognising a food allergy is difficult. Humans vomit or have rashes when they eat a food to which they are allergic. Dogs neither vomit nor (usually) develop rashes. They react in the same manner as they would to an airborne or flea allergy; they itch, scratch and bite, thus making the diagnosis extremely difficult. While pollen allergies and parasite bites are usually seasonal, food allergies are year-round problems.

### FOOD INTOLERANCE

Food intolerance is the inability of the dog to completely digest certain foods. For example, puppies that may have done very well on their mother's milk may not do well on cow's milk. The results of food intolerance may be evident in loose bowels, passing gas and stomach pains. These are the only obvious symptoms of food intolerance, which makes diagnosis difficult.

### TREATING FOOD PROBLEMS

It is possible to handle food allergies and food intolerance yourself. Start by putting your dog on a diet that he has never had. Obviously, if the dog has never eaten this new food, he can't have been allergic or intolerant of it. Start with a single ingredient that is not in the dog's diet at the present time. Ingredients like chopped beef or fish are common in dogs' diets, so try something more exotic like rabbit, pheasant or even just vegetables. Keep the dog on this diet (with no additives) for a month. If the symptoms of food allergy or intolerance disappear, it is quite likely that your dog has a food allergy.

Don't think that the single ingredient cured the problem. You still must find a suitable diet and ascertain which ingredient in the old diet was objectionable. This is most easily done by adding ingredients to the new diet one at a time. Let the dog stay on the modified diet for a month before you add another ingredient. Eventually, you will determine the ingredient that caused the adverse reaction.

An alternative method is to carefully study the ingredients in the diet to which your dog is allergic or intolerant. Identify the main ingredient in this diet and eliminate the main ingredient by buying a different food that does not have that ingredient. Keep experimenting until the symptoms disappear after one month on the new diet.

## EXTERNAL PARASITES

### FLEAS

Of all the problems to which dogs are prone, none is more well known and frustrating than fleas. Flea infestation is relatively simple to cure but difficult to prevent. Parasites that are harboured inside the body are a bit more difficult to eradicate but they are easier to control.

To control flea infestation, you have to understand the flea's life cycle. Fleas are often thought of as a summertime problem, but centrally heated homes have changed the patterns and fleas can be found at any time of the year. The most effective method of flea control is a two-stage approach: one stage to kill the adult fleas, and the other to control the development of pre-adult fleas. Unfortunately, no single active ingredient is effective against all stages of the life cycle.

### LIFE CYCLE STAGES

During its life, a flea will pass through four life stages: egg, larva, pupa and adult. The adult stage is the most visible and irritating stage of the flea life cycle, and this is

Magnified head
of a dog flea,
*Ctenocephalides
canis.*

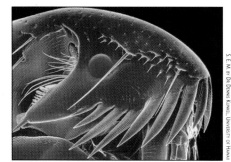

S. E. M. BY DR DENNIS KUNKEL, UNIVESITY OF HAWAII

A male dog flea,
*Ctenocephalides
canis.*

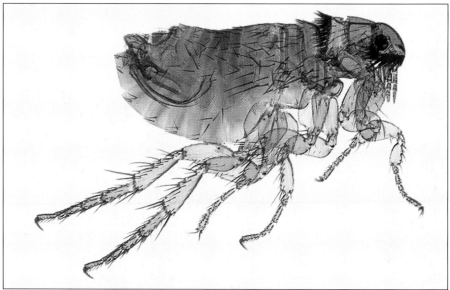

PHOTO BY JEAN CLAUDE REVY/PHOTOTAKE

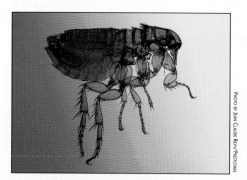

Photo by Jean Claude Revy/Phototake

## A LOOK AT FLEAS

Fleas have been around for millions of years and have adapted to changing host animals. They are able to go through a complete life cycle in less than one month or they can extend their lives to almost two years by remaining as pupae or cocoons. They do not need blood or any other food for up to 20 months.

They have been measured as being able to jump 300,000 times and can jump 150 times their length in any direction, including straight up. Those are just a few of the reasons why they are so successful in infesting a dog!

why the majority of flea-control products concentrate on this stage. The fact is that adult fleas account for only 1% of the total flea population, and the other 99% exist in pre-adult stages, i.e. eggs, larvae and pupae. The pre-adult stages are barely visible to the naked eye.

### THE LIFE CYCLE OF THE FLEA

Eggs are laid on the dog, usually in quantities of about 20 or 30, several times a day. The female adult flea must have a blood meal before each egg-laying session. When first laid, the eggs will cling to the dog's hair, as the eggs are still moist. However, they will quickly dry out and fall from the dog, especially if the dog moves around or scratches. Many eggs will fall off in the dog's favourite area or an area in which he spends a lot of time, such as his bed.

Once the eggs fall from the dog onto the carpet or furniture, they will hatch into larvae. This takes from one to ten days. Larvae are not particularly mobile and will usually travel only a few inches

# The Life Cycle of the Flea

**Eggs**

**Larvae**

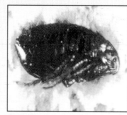

**Pupa**

**Adult**

Photos courtesy of Fleabusters® R_x for fleas.

from where they hatch. However, they do have a tendency to move away from light and heavy traffic—under furniture and behind doors are common places to find high quantities of flea larvae.

The flea larvae feed on dead organic matter, including adult flea faeces, until they are ready to change into adult fleas. Fleas will usually remain as larvae for around seven days. After this period, the larvae will pupate into protective pupae. While inside the pupae, the larvae will undergo metamorphosis and change into adult fleas. This can take as little time as a few days, but the adult fleas can remain inside the pupae waiting to hatch for up to two years. The pupae are signalled to hatch by certain stimuli, such as physical pressure—the pupae's being stepped on, heat from an animal lying on the pupae or increased carbon dioxide levels and vibrations—indicating that a suitable host is available.

## FLEA KILLERS

Flea-killers are poisonous. You should not spray these toxic chemicals on areas of a dog's body that he licks, on his genitals or on his face. Flea killers taken internally are a better answer, but check with your vet in case internal therapy is not advised for your dog.

## INSECT GROWTH REGULATOR (IGR)

Two types of products should be used when treating fleas—a product to treat the pet and a product to treat the home. Adult fleas represent less than 1% of the flea population. The pre-adult fleas (eggs, larvae and pupae) represent more than 99% of the flea population and are found in the environment; it is in the case of pre-adult fleas that products containing an Insect Growth Regulator (IGR) should be used in the home.

IGRs are a new class of compounds used to prevent the development of insects. They do not kill the insect outright, but instead use the insect's biology against it to stop it from completing its growth. Products that contain methoprene are the world's first and leading IGRs. Used to control fleas and other insects, this type of IGR will stop flea larvae from developing and protect the house for up to seven months.

Once hatched, the adult flea must feed within a few days. Once the adult flea finds a host, it will not leave voluntarily. It only becomes dislodged by grooming or the host animal's scratching. The adult flea will remain on the host for the duration of its life unless forcibly removed.

PHOTO BY DWIGHT R KUHN

Dwight R Kuhn's magnificent action photo, showing a flea jumping from a dog's back.

### TREATING THE ENVIRONMENT AND THE DOG

Treating fleas should be a two-pronged attack. First, the environment needs to be treated; this includes carpets and furniture, especially the dog's bedding and areas underneath furniture. The environment should be treated with a household spray containing an Insect Growth Regulator (IGR) and an insecticide to kill the adult fleas. Most IGRs are effective against eggs and larvae; they actually mimic the fleas' own hormones and stop the eggs and larvae from developing into adult fleas. There are currently no treatments available to attack the pupa stage of the life cycle, so the adult insecticide is used to kill the newly hatched adult fleas before they find a host. Most IGRs are active for many months, while adult insecticides are only active for a few days.

A scanning electron micrograph (S. E. M.) of a dog flea, *Ctenocephalides canis.*

S. E. M. BY DR DENNIS KUNKEL, UNIVERSITY OF HAWAII

When treating with a household spray, it is a good idea to vacuum before applying the product. This stimulates as many pupae as possible to hatch into adult fleas. The vacuum cleaner should also be treated with an insecticide to prevent the eggs and larvae that have been hoovered into the vacuum bag from hatching.

The second stage of treatment is to apply an adult insecticide to the dog. Traditionally, this would be in the form of a collar or a spray, but more recent innovations include digestible insecticides that poison the fleas when they ingest the dog's blood. Alternatively, there are drops that, when placed on the back of the animal's neck, spread throughout the fur and skin to kill adult fleas.

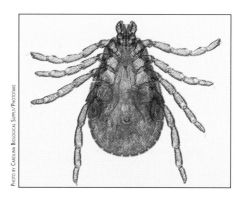

A brown dog tick, *Rhipicephalus sanguineus*, is an uncommon but annoying tick found on dogs.

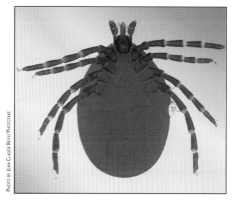

An uncommon dog tick of the genus *Ixode*. Magnified 10x.

## TICKS AND MITES

Though not as common as fleas, ticks and mites are found all over the tropical and temperate world. They don't bite, like fleas; they harpoon. They dig their sharp proboscis (nose) into the dog's skin and drink the blood. Their only food and drink is dog's blood. Dogs can get Lyme disease, Rocky Mountain spotted fever (normally found in the US only), paralysis and many other diseases from ticks and mites. They may live where fleas are

The head of a dog tick, *Dermacentor variabilis*, enlarged and coloured for effect.

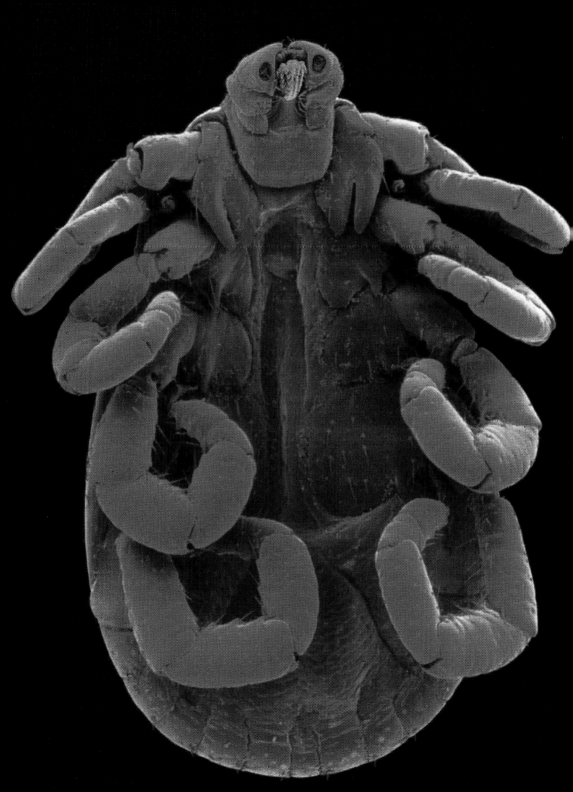

PHOTO BY DWIGHT R KUHN

**Human lice look like dog lice and the two are closely related.**

S. E. M. BY DR ANDREW SYELMAN / PHOTOTAKE.

## BEWARE THE DEER TICK

The great outdoors may be fun for your dog, but it also is a home to dangerous ticks. Deer ticks carry a bacterium known as *Borrelia burgdorferi* and are most active in the autumn and spring. When infections are caught early, penicillin and tetracycline are effective antibiotics, but if left untreated the bacteria may cause neurological, kidney and cardiac problems as well as long-term trouble with walking and painful joints.

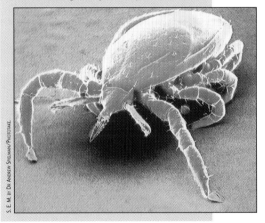

found and they like to hide in cracks or seams in walls wherever dogs live. They are controlled the same way fleas are controlled.

The dog tick, *Dermacentor variabilis*, may well be the most common dog tick in many geographical areas, especially those areas where the climate is hot and humid.

Most dog ticks have life expectancies of a week to six months, depending upon climatic conditions. They can neither jump nor fly, but they can crawl slowly and can range up to 5 metres (16 feet) to reach a sleeping or unsuspecting dog.

### MANGE

Mites cause a skin irritation called mange. Some are contagious, like *Cheyletiella*, ear mites, scabies and chiggers. Mites that cause ear-mite infestations are usually controlled with Lindane, which can only be

**Opposite page:**
The dog tick, *Dermacentor variabilis*, is probably the most common tick found on dogs. Look at the strength in its eight legs! No wonder it's hard to detach them.

The mange mite, *Psoroptes bovis*.

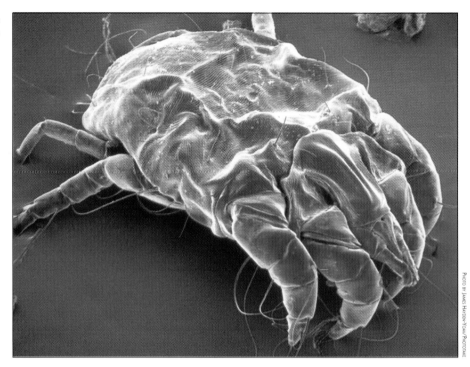

PHOTO BY JAMES HAYDEN-YOAV/PHOTOTAKE

The roundworm, *Rhabditis*. The roundworm can infect both dogs and humans.

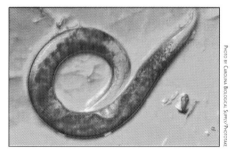

PHOTO BY CAROLINA BIOLOGICAL SUPPLY/PHOTOTAKE

The common roundworm, *Ascaris lumbricoides*.

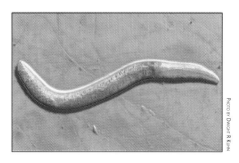

PHOTO BY DWIGHT R KUHN

administered by a vet, followed by Tresaderm at home.

It is essential that your dog be treated for mange as quickly as possible because some forms of mange are transmissible to people.

**INTERNAL PARASITES**

Most animals—fishes, birds and mammals, including dogs and humans—have worms and other parasites that live inside their bodies. According to Dr Herbert R Axelrod, the fish pathologist, there are two kinds of parasites: dumb and smart. The smart parasites live in peaceful cooperation with their hosts (symbiosis), while the dumb parasites kill their hosts. Most of the worm infections are relatively easy to control. If they are not controlled, they weaken the host dog to the point that other medical problems occur, but they are not dumb parasites.

## ROUNDWORMS

The roundworms that infect dogs are scientifically known as *Toxocara canis*. They live in the dog's intestines. The worms shed eggs continually. It has been estimated that a dog produces about 150 grammes of faeces every day. Each gramme of faeces

### ROUNDWORMS

Average size dogs can pass 1,360,000 roundworm eggs every day. For example, if there were only 1 million dogs in the world, the world would be saturated with 1,300 metric tonnes of dog faeces. These faeces would contain 15,000,000,000 roundworm eggs.

Up to 31% of home gardens and children's play boxes in the US contain roundworm eggs.

Flushing dog's faeces down the toilet is not a safe practice because the usual sewage treatments do not destroy roundworm eggs.

Infected puppies start shedding roundworm eggs at 3 weeks of age. They can be infected by their mother's milk.

### DEWORMING

Ridding your puppy of worms is *very important* because certain worms that puppies carry, such as tapeworms and roundworms, can infect humans.

Breeders initiate deworming programmes at or about four weeks of age. The routine is repeated every two or three weeks until the puppy is three months old. The breeder from whom you obtained your puppy should provide you with the complete details of the deworming programme.

Your veterinary surgeon can prescribe and monitor the programme of deworming for you. The usual programme is treating the puppy every 15–20 days until the puppy is positively worm-free. It is advised that you only treat your puppy with drugs that are recommended professionally.

averages 10,000–12,000 eggs of roundworms. There are no known areas in which dogs roam that do not contain roundworm eggs. The greatest danger of roundworms is that they infect people too! It is wise to have your dog tested regularly for roundworms.

Pigs also have roundworm infections that can be passed to humans and dogs. The typical roundworm parasite is called *Ascaris lumbricoides*.

Left: The roundworm *Rhabditis.* Right: Male and female hookworms. *Ancylostoma caninum* are uncommonly found in pet or show dogs in Britain.

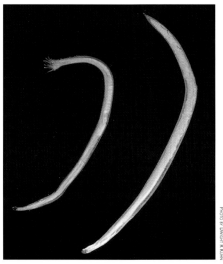

PHOTO BY DWIGHT R KUHN

PHOTO BY DWIGHT R KUHN

## HOOKWORMS

The worm *Ancylostoma caninum* is commonly called the dog hookworm. It is also dangerous to humans and cats. It has teeth by which it attaches itself to the intestines of the dog. It changes the site of its attachment about six times a day and the dog loses blood from each detachment, possibly causing iron-deficiency anaemia. Hookworms are easily purged from the dog with many medications. Milbemycin oxime, which also serves as a heartworm

The infective stage of the hookworm larva.

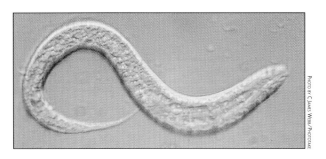

PHOTO BY C JAMES WEBB/PHOTOTAKE

preventative in Collies, can be used for this purpose.

In Britain the 'temperate climate' hookworm (*Uncinaria stenocephala*) is rarely found in pet or show dogs, but can occur in hunting packs, racing Greyhounds and sheepdogs because the worms can be prevalent wherever dogs are exercised regularly on grassland.

## TAPEWORMS

There are many species of tapeworm. They are carried by fleas! The dog eats the flea and starts the tapeworm cycle. Humans can also be infected with tapeworms, so don't eat fleas! Fleas are so small that your dog could pass them onto your hands, your plate or your food and thus make it possible for you to ingest a flea that is carrying tapeworm eggs.

While tapeworm infection is

Heartworm, *Dirofilaria immitis.*

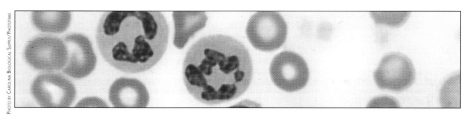

Magnified heartworm larvae, *Dirofilaria immitis.*

not life-threatening in dogs (smart parasite!), it can be the cause of a very serious liver disease for humans. About 50 percent of the humans infected with *Echinococcus multilocularis,* a type of tapeworm that causes alveolar hydatis, perish.

## TAPEWORMS

Humans, rats, squirrels, foxes, coyotes, wolves and domestic dogs are all susceptible to tapeworm infection. Except in humans, tapeworms are usually not a fatal infection. Infected individuals can harbour a thousand parasitic worms.

Tapeworms have two sexes—male and female (many other worms have only one sex—male and female in the same worm).

If dogs eat infected rats or mice, they get the tapeworm disease. One month after attaching to a dog's intestine, the worm starts shedding eggs. These eggs are infective immediately. Infective eggs can live for a few months without a host animal.

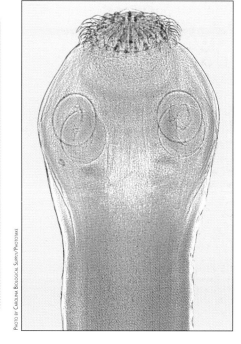

The head and rostellum (the round prominence on the scolex) of a tapeworm, which infects dogs and humans.

The heart of a dog infected with canine heartworm, *Dirofilaria immitis.*

PHOTO BY JAMES E HAYDEN, RPB/PHOTOTAKE

### HEARTWORMS

Heartworms are thin, extended worms up to 30 cms (12 ins) long, which live in a dog's heart and the major blood vessels surrounding it. Dogs may have up to 200 worms. Symptoms may be loss of energy, loss of appetite, coughing, the development of a pot belly and anaemia.

Heartworms are transmitted by mosquitoes. The mosquito drinks the blood of an infected dog and takes in larvae with the blood. The larvae, called microfilaria, develop within the body of the mosquito and are passed on to the next dog bitten after the larvae mature. It takes two to three weeks for the larvae to develop to the infective stage within the body of the mosquito. Dogs should be treated at about six weeks of age, and maintained on a prophylactic dose given monthly.

Blood testing for heartworms is not necessarily indicative of how seriously your dog is infected. This is a dangerous disease. Although heartworm is a problem for dogs in America, Australia, Asia and Central Europe, dogs in the United Kingdom are not currently affected by heartworm.

# First Aid at a Glance

### Burns
Place the affected area under cool water; use ice if only a small area is burnt.

### Bee/Insect bites
Apply ice to relieve swelling; antihistamine dosed properly.

### Animal bites
Clean any bleeding area; apply pressure until bleeding subsides; go to the vet.

### Spider bites
Use cold compress and a pressurised pack to inhibit venom's spreading.

### Antifreeze poisoning
Induce vomiting with hydrogen peroxide. Seek *immediate* veterinary help!

### Fish hooks
Removal best handled by vet; hook must be cut in order to remove.

### Snake bites
Pack ice around bite; contact vet quickly; identify snake for proper antivenin.

### Car accident
Move dog from roadway with blanket; seek veterinary aid.

### Shock
Calm the dog, keep him warm; seek immediate veterinary help.

### Nosebleed
Apply cold compress to the nose; apply pressure to any visible abrasion.

### Bleeding
Apply pressure above the area; treat wound by applying a cotton pack.

### Heat stroke
Submerge dog in cold bath; cool down with fresh air and water; go to the vet.

### Frostbite/Hypothermia
Warm the dog with a warm bath, electric blankets or hot water bottles.

### Abrasions
Clean the wound and wash out thoroughly with fresh water; apply antiseptic.

 *Remember: an injured dog may attempt to bite a helping hand from fear and confusion. Always muzzle the dog before trying to offer assistance.*

# CDS: COGNITIVE DYSFUNCTION SYNDROME
## 'OLD-DOG SYNDROME'

There are many ways to evaluate old-dog syndrome. Veterinary surgeons have defined CDS (cognitive dysfunction syndrome) as the gradual deterioration of cognitive abilities. These are indicated by changes in the dog's behaviour. When a dog changes its routine response, and maladies have been eliminated as the cause of these behavioural changes, then CDS is the usual diagnosis.

More than half the dogs over eight years old suffer from some form of CDS. The older the dog, the more chance it has of suffering from CDS. In humans, doctors often dismiss the CDS behavioural changes as part of 'winding down.'

There are four major signs of CDS: the dog has frequent toilet accidents inside the home, sleeps much more or much less than normal, acts confused and fails to respond to social stimuli.

## SYMPTOMS OF CDS

### FREQUENT TOILET ACCIDENTS
- Urinates in the house.
- Defecates in the house.
- Doesn't signal that he wants to go out.

### SLEEP PATTERNS
- Moves much more slowly.
- Sleeps more than normal during the day.
- Sleeps less during the night.

### CONFUSION
- Goes outside and just stands there.
- Appears confused with a faraway look in his eyes.
- Hides more often.
- Doesn't recognise friends.
- Doesn't come when called.
- Walks around listlessly and without a destination.

### FAILS TO RESPOND TO SOCIAL STIMULI
- Comes to people less frequently, whether called or not.
- Doesn't tolerate petting for more than a short time.
- Doesn't come to the door when you return home.

## Your Veteran

# DEERHOUND

The term *old* is a qualitative term. For dogs as well as for their masters, old is relative. Certainly we can all distinguish between a puppy Deerhound and an adult Deerhound—there are the obvious physical traits, such as size, appearance and facial expressions, and personality traits. Puppies and young dogs like to play with children. Children's natural exuberance is a good match for the seemingly endless energy of young dogs. They like to run, jump, chase and retrieve. When dogs grow older and cease their interaction with children, they are often thought of as being too old to keep pace with the kids. On the other hand, if a Deerhound is only exposed to older people or quieter lifestyles, his life will normally be less active and the decrease in his activity level as he ages will not be as obvious.

If people live to be 100 years old, dogs live to be 20 years old. While this might seem like a good rule of thumb, it is very inaccurate. When trying to compare dog years to human years, you cannot make a generalisation about all dogs. You can make the generali-

sation that 10 or 11 years is a good lifespan for a Deerhound, which is quite reasonable given the size of the breed. Unfortunately, the large-breed dogs never live as long as the smaller toy dogs, though the Deerhound is long-lived for a dog of his inches!

Deerhounds are considered physically mature at about 18 months, though some breeds take as long as 3 years to mature. The general rule is that the first 3 years of a dog's life are like 7

---

### SENIOR SIGNS

An old dog starts to show one or more of the following symptoms:

• The hair on the face and paws starts to turn grey. The colour breakdown usually starts around the eyes and mouth.

• Sleep patterns are deeper and longer, and the old dog is harder to awaken.

• Food intake diminishes.

• Responses to calls, whistles and other signals are ignored more and more.

• Eye contact does not evoke tail wagging (assuming it once did).

A veteran Deerhound still looking happy, healthy and in good condition.

times that of comparable humans. That means a 3-year-old dog is like a 21-year-old human. As the curve of comparison shows, there is no hard and fast rule for comparing dog and human ages. Some breeds' adolescent periods last longer than others' and some breeds experience rapid periods of growth. The comparison is made even more difficult, for, likewise, not all humans age at the same rate...and human females live longer than human males.

## WHAT TO LOOK FOR IN VETERANS

Most veterinary surgeons and behaviourists use the seven-year mark as the time to consider a dog a 'veteran' or a 'senior.' The term does not imply that the dog is geriatric and has begun to fail in mind and body. Ageing is essentially a slowing process. Humans readily admit that they

feel a difference in their activity level from age 20 to 30, and then from 30 to 40, etc. By treating the seven-year-old dog as a veteran, owners are able to implement certain therapeutic and preventative medical strategies with the help of their veterinary surgeons. A senior-care programme should include at least two veterinary visits per year and screening sessions to determine the dog's health status, as well as nutritional counselling. Veterinary surgeons determine the senior dog's health status through a blood smear for a complete blood count, serum chemistry profile with electrolytes, urinalysis, blood pressure check, electrocardiogram, ocular tonometry (pressure on the eyeball) and dental prophylaxis.

Such an extensive programme for senior dogs is well advised before owners start to see the obvious physical signs of ageing, such as slower and inhibited movement, greying, increased sleep/nap periods and disinterest in play and other activity. This preventative programme promises a longer, healthier life for the ageing dog. Among the physical problems common in ageing dogs are the loss of sight and hearing, arthritis, kidney and liver failure, diabetes mellitus, heart disease and Cushing's disease (an hormonal disease).

In addition to the physical

manifestations discussed, there are some behavioural changes and problems related to ageing dogs. Dogs suffering from hearing or vision loss, dental discomfort or arthritis can become aggressive. Likewise, the near-deaf and/or blind dog may be startled more easily and react in an unexpectedly aggressive manner. Seniors suffering from senility can become more impatient and irritable. Housesoiling accidents are associated with loss of mobility, kidney problems and loss of sphincter control as well as plaque accumulation, physiological brain changes and reactions to medications. Older dogs, just like young puppies, suffer from separation anxiety, which can lead to excessive barking, whining, housesoiling and destructive

behaviour. Seniors may become fearful of everyday sounds, such as vacuum cleaners, heaters, thunder and passing traffic. Some dogs have difficulty sleeping, due to discomfort, the need for frequent toilet visits and the like.

Owners should avoid spoiling the older dog with too many fatty treats. Obesity is a common problem in older dogs and subtracts years from their lives. Keep the senior dog as trim as possible, since excessive weight puts additional stress on the body's vital organs. Some breeders recommend supplementing the diet with foods high in fibre and lower in calories. Adding fresh vegetables and marrow broth to the senior's diet makes a tasty, low-calorie, low-fat supplement. Vets also offer speciality diets for senior dogs that are worth exploring.

Your dog, as he nears his twilight years, needs your

Some dogs never lose their curiosity, even as seniors! This veteran inspects the garden landscaping.

patience and good care more than ever. Never punish an older dog for an accident or abnormal behaviour. For all the years of love, protection and companionship that your dog has provided, he deserves special attention and courtesies. The older dog may need to relieve himself at 3 a.m. because he can no longer hold it for eight hours. Older dogs may not be able to remain crated for more than two or three hours. It may be time to give up a sofa or chair to your old friend. Although he may not seem as enthusiastic about your attention and petting, he does appreciate the considerations you offer as he gets older.

Your Deerhound does not understand why his world is slowing down. Owners must make their dogs' transition into their golden years as pleasant and rewarding as possible.

## WHAT TO DO WHEN THE TIME COMES

You are never fully prepared to make a rational decision about putting your dog to sleep. It is very obvious that you love your Deerhound or you would not be reading this book. Putting a beloved dog to sleep is extremely difficult. It is a decision that must be made with your veterinary surgeon. You are usually forced to make the decision when your dog experiences one or more life-threatening symptoms that have become serious enough for you to seek medical (veterinary) help.

If the prognosis of the malady indicates that the end is near and that your beloved pet will only continue to suffer and experience no enjoyment for the balance of its life, then euthanasia is the right choice.

### WHAT IS EUTHANASIA?

Euthanasia derives from the Greek, meaning *good death*. In other words, it means the planned, painless killing of a dog suffering from a painful, incurable condition, or who is so aged that it cannot walk, see, eat or control its excretory functions. Euthanasia is usually accomplished by injection with an overdose of anaesthesia or a barbiturate. Aside from the prick of the needle, the experience is usually painless.

### MAKING THE DECISION

The decision to euthanise your dog is never easy. The days during which the dog becomes ill and the end occurs can be unusually stressful for you. If this is your first experience with the death of a loved one, you may need the comfort dictated by your religious beliefs. If you are the head of the family and have children, you should have involved them in the decision of putting your Deerhound to sleep. Usually your dog can be maintained on drugs for a few days in order to give you ample time to make a decision. During this time, talking with members of your family or with people who have lived through the same experience can ease the burden of your inevitable decision.

### THE FINAL RESTING PLACE

Dogs can have some of the same privileges as humans. The remains of your beloved dog can be buried in a pet cemetery, which is generally expensive. Dogs who have died at home can be buried in your garden in a place suitably marked with some stone or newly planted tree or bush. Alternatively, your dog can be cremated individually and the ashes returned to you. A less expensive option is mass cremation, although, of course, the ashes cannot then be returned. Vets can usually arrange the cremation on your behalf. The cost of these options should always be discussed frankly and openly with your veterinary surgeon. In Britain, if your dog has died at the surgery, the vet legally cannot allow you to take your dog's body home.

### GETTING ANOTHER DOG?

The grief of losing your beloved dog will be as lasting as the grief of losing a human friend or relative. In most cases, if your dog died of old age (if there is such a thing), it had slowed down

---

**COPING WITH LOSS**

When your dog dies, you may be as upset as when a human companion passes away. You are losing your protector, your baby, your confidante and your best friend. Many people experience not only grief but also feelings of guilt and doubt as to whether they did all that they could for their pet. Allow yourself to grieve and mourn, and seek help from friends and support groups. You may also wish to consult books and websites that deal with this topic.

---

considerably. Do you want a new Deerhound puppy to replace it? Or are you better off finding a more mature Deerhound, say two to three years of age, which will usually be house-trained and will have an already developed personality. In this case, you can find out if you like each other after a few hours of being together.

The decision is, of course, your own. Do you want another Deerhound or perhaps a different breed so as to avoid comparison with your beloved friend? Most people usually buy the same breed because they know (and love) the characteristics of that breed. Then, too, they often know people who have the same breed and perhaps they are lucky enough that one of their friends expects a litter soon. What could be better?

# *Showing Your*
# DEERHOUND

When you purchase your Deerhound, you will make it clear to the breeder whether you want one just as a loveable companion and pet, or if you hope to be buying a Deerhound with show prospects. No reputable breeder will sell you a young puppy and tell you that it is *definitely* of show quality, for so much can go wrong during the early months of a puppy's development. If you plan to show, what you will hopefully have acquired is a puppy with 'show potential.'

To the novice, exhibiting a Deerhound in the show ring may look easy, but it takes a lot of hard work and devotion to do top winning at a show such as the prestigious Crufts Dog Show, not to mention a little luck too!

The first concept that the canine novice learns when watching a dog show is that each dog first competes against members of its own breed. Once the judge has selected the best member of each breed (Best of Breed), provided that the show is judged on a Group system, that chosen dog will compete with other dogs in its group. Finally,

## INFORMATION ON CLUBS

You can get information about dog shows from kennel clubs and breed clubs:

Fédération Cynologique Internationale
14, rue Leopold II, B-6530 Thuin, Belgium
www.fci.be

The Kennel Club
1-5 Clarges St., Piccadilly, London W1Y 8AB, UK
www.the-kennel-club.org.uk

American Kennel Club
5580 Centerview Dr., Raleigh, NC 27606-3390 USA
www.akc.org

Canadian Kennel Club
89 Skyway Ave., Suite 100, Etobicoke, Ontario
M9W 6R4 Canada
www.ckc.ca

the best of each group will compete for Best in Show and Reserve Best in Show.

The second concept that you must understand is that the dogs are not actually compared against one another. The judge compares each dog against its breed standard, which is a written description of the ideal specimen of the breed. While some early breed standards were indeed based on specific dogs that were famous or popular, many dedicated enthusiasts say that a perfect specimen, as described in the standard, has never walked into a show ring, has never been bred and, to the woe of dog breeders around the globe, does not exist. Breeders attempt to get as close to this ideal as possible with every litter, but theoretically the 'perfect' dog is so elusive that it is impossible. (And if the 'perfect' dog were born, breeders and judges would never agree that it was indeed 'perfect.')

If you are interested in exploring the world of dog showing, your best bet is to join your local breed club. These clubs often host both Championship and Open Shows, and sometimes Match meetings and special events, all of which could be of interest even if you are only an onlooker. Clubs also send out newsletters, and some organise training days and seminars in order that people may learn more about their chosen breed. To locate the breed club closest to you, contact The Kennel Club, the ruling body for the British dog world. The Kennel Club governs not only conformation shows but also working trials, obedience shows, agility trials and field trials. The Kennel Club furnishes the rules and regulations for all of

Dogs in the show ring are 'stacked,' meaning that they stand in a position to show them off to their best advantage.

these events plus general dog registration and other basic requirements of dog ownership. Its annual show, called the Crufts Dog Show, held in Birmingham, is the largest benched show in England. Every year over 20,000 of the UK's best dogs qualify to participate in this marvellous show, which lasts four days.

The Kennel Club governs many different kinds of shows in Great Britain, Australia, South Africa and beyond. At the most competitive and prestigious of these shows, the Championship Shows, a dog can earn Challenge Certificates (CCs), and thereby become a Show Champion or a Champion. A dog must earn three Challenge Certificates under three different judges to earn the prefix of 'Sh Ch' or 'Ch.' Some breeds must also qualify in a field trial in order to gain the title of full Champion. Challenge Certificates are awarded to a very small percentage of the dogs competing, and dogs that are already

Champions compete with others for these coveted CCs. The number of Challenge Certificates awarded in any one year is based upon the total number of dogs in each breed entered for competition.

There are three types of Championship Shows: an all-breed General Championship Show for all Kennel-Club-recognised breeds; a Group Championship Show, which is limited to breeds within one of the groups; and a Breed Show, which is usually confined to a single breed. The Kennel Club determines which breeds at which Championship Shows will have the opportunity to earn Challenge Certificates (or tickets). Serious exhibitors often will opt not to participate if the tickets are withheld at a particular show. This policy makes earning championships even more difficult to accomplish.

Open Shows are generally less competitive and are frequently

**An interesting class is the brace class, in which nearly identical dogs compete in pairs. These braces and their handlers take a turn around the ring for the judge.**

used as 'practice shows' for young dogs. There are hundreds of Open Shows each year that can be delightful social events and are great first show experiences for the novice. Even if you're considering just watching a show to wet your paws, an Open Show is a great choice.

While Championship and Open Shows are most important for the beginner to understand, there are other types of shows in which the interested dog owner can participate. Training clubs sponsor Matches that can be entered on the day of the show for a nominal fee. In these introductory-level exhibitions, two dogs' names are pulled out of a hat and 'matched,' the winner of that match goes on to the next round and eventually only one dog is left undefeated.

Exemption Shows are much more light-hearted affairs with usually only four pedigree classes and several 'fun' classes, all of which can be entered on the day of the show. Exemption Shows are sometimes held in conjunction with small agricultural shows and the proceeds must be given to a charity. Limited Shows are also available in small number. Entry is restricted to members of the club that hosts the show, although one can usually join the club when making an entry.

Before you actually step into the ring, you would be well

## SHOW QUALITY SHOWS

While you may purchase a puppy in the hope of having a successful career in the show ring, it is impossible to tell, at eight to ten weeks of age, whether your dog will be a contender. Some promising pups end up with minor to serious faults that prevent them from taking home a Best of Breed award, but this certainly does not mean they can't be the best of companions for you and your family. To find out if your potential show dog is show quality, enter him in a match to see how a judge evaluates him. You may also take him back to your breeder as he matures to see what he might advise.

advised to sit back and observe the judge's ring procedure. If it is your first time in the ring, do not be over-anxious and run to the front of the line. It is much better to stand back and study how the exhibitor in front of you is performing. The judge asks each handler to 'stand' the dog, hopefully showing the dog off to his best advantage. The judge will observe the dog from a distance and from different angles, and approach the dog to check his teeth, overall structure, alertness and muscle tone, as well as consider how well the dog 'conforms' to the standard. Most importantly, the judge will have the exhibitor move the dog around the ring in some pattern that he or she should specify (another advantage to not going first, but always listen since some judges change their directions—and the judge is always right!). Finally, the judge will give the dog one last look before moving on to the next exhibitor.

*As the handler presents his Deerhound in front of the judging table, the judge reviews the dog and makes notes.*

> ### SEVEN GROUPS
> The Kennel Club divides its dogs into seven Groups: Gundog, Utility, Working, Toy, Terrier, Hound and Pastoral.*
>
> *\*The Pastoral Group, established in 1999, includes those sheepdog breeds previously categorised in the Working Group.*

If you are not in the top three at your first show, do not be discouraged. Be patient and consistent, and you may eventually find yourself in the winning line-up. Remember that the winners were once in your shoes and have devoted many hours and much money to earn the placement. If you find that your dog is losing every time and never getting a nod, it may be time to consider a different dog sport or to just enjoy your Deerhound as a pet.

Virtually all countries with a recognised speciality breed club (sometimes called a 'parent' club) offer show conformation competition specifically for and among Deerhounds. Under direction of the club, other special events for coursing, tracking, obedience and agility may be offered as well, whether for titling or just for fun.

### WORKING TRIALS
Working trials can be entered by any well-trained dog of any breed, not just Gundogs or Working dogs.

The judge reviews the line of Deerhounds, examining each dog individually. As well as looking at each dog's overall appearance, she feels for correct bone structure.

Many dogs that earn the Kennel Club Good Citizen Dog award choose to participate in a working trial. There are five stakes at both Open and Championship levels: Companion Dog (CD), Utility Dog (UD), Working Dog (WD), Tracking Dog (TD) and Patrol Dog (PD). As in conformation shows, dogs compete against a standard and, if the dog reaches the qualifying mark, it obtains a certificate. The exercises are divided into groups, and the dog must achieve at least 70 percent of the allotted score for each exercise in order to qualify. If the dog achieves 80 percent in the Open level, it receives a Certificate of Merit (COM); in the Championship level, it receives a Qualifying Certificate. At the CD stake, dogs must participate in four groups: Control, Stay, Agility and Search (Retrieve and Nosework). At the next three levels, UD, WD and TD, there are only three groups: Control, Agility and Nosework.

The Agility exercises consist of three jumps: a vertical scale up a six-foot wall of planks; a clear jump over a basic three-foot hurdle with a removable top bar; and a long jump across angled planks stretching nine feet.

To earn the UD, WD and TD, dogs must track approximately one-half mile for articles laid from one-half hour to three hours previously. Tracks consist of turns and legs, and fresh ground is used for each participant. The fifth stake, PD, involves teaching manwork, which is not recommended for every breed.

## AGILITY TRIALS
Agility trials began in Britain in 1977 and have since spread around the world, especially to

the United States, where they are very popular. While many members of the Hound Group participate in agility trials, surprisingly not too many Deerhounds do. Though, this is not to say that the breed would not do well if the proper training were utilised.

In an agility trial, the handler directs his dog over an obstacle course that includes jumps (such as those used in the working trials), as well as tyres, the dog walk, weave poles, pipe tunnels, collapsed tunnels, etc. The Kennel Club requires that dogs not be trained for agility until they are 12 months old. This dog sport is great fun for dog and owner, and interested owners should join a training club that has obstacles and experienced agility handlers who can introduce you and your dog to the 'ropes' (and tyres, tunnels, etc.).

## SIGHTHOUND TRIALS AND EVENTS

In Britain, coursing events and lure coursing trials are organised by the National Coursing Club, and Deerhounds are regular participants. If you are interested in finding out more about these trials and other events that attract sighthound enthusiasts, such as dog racing, contact your local Deerhound club or The Kennel Club for more information. Most of these events do not require as

much preparation as other formal competitive events, and Deerhounds respond naturally to the task at hand. You will be invigorated by watching your talented coursing dog doing what his ancestors were bred to do!

## FÉDÉRATION CYNOLOGIQUE INTERNATIONALE

Established in 1911, the Fédération Cynologique Internationale (FCI) represents the 'world kennel club.' This international body brings uniformity to the breeding, judging and showing of pure-bred dogs. Although the FCI originally included only five European nations: France, Germany, Austria, the Netherlands and Belgium (which remains its headquarters), the organisation today embraces nations on six continents and recognises well over 300 breeds of pure-bred dog.

FCI sponsors both national and international shows. The hosting country determines the judging system and breed standards are always based on the breed's country of origin. Dogs from every country can participate in these impressive canine spectacles, the largest of which is the World Dog Show, hosted in a different country each year.

There are three titles attainable through the FCI: the International Champion, which is the most prestigious; the

International Beauty Champion, which is based on aptitude certificates in different countries; and the International Trial Champion, which is based on achievement in obedience trials in different countries. The title of Champion at an FCI show requires a dog to win three CACs (*Certificats d'Aptitude au Championnat*), at regional or club shows under three different judges who are breed specialists. The title of International Champion is gained by winning four CACIBs (*Certificats d'Aptitude au Championnat International de Beauté*), which are offered only at international shows, with at least a one-year lapse between the first and fourth award.

The FCI is divided into ten 'Groups.' At the World Dog Show, the following 'Classes' are offered for each breed: Puppy Class (6–9 months), Youth Class (9–18 months), Open Class (15 months or older) and Champion Class. A dog can be awarded a classification of Excellent, Very Good, Good, Sufficient and Not Sufficient. Puppies can be awarded classifications of Very Promising, Promising or Not Promising. Four placements are made in each class. After all classes are judged, a Best of Breed is selected. Other special groups and classes may also be shown. Each exhibitor showing a dog receives a written evaluation from the judge.

Besides the World Dog Show and other all-breed shows, you can exhibit your dog at speciality shows held by different breed clubs. Speciality shows may have their own regulations.

Whether or not you go home a winner, showing should be an enjoyable activity for all participants, human and canine.

# DEERHOUND

As a Deerhound owner, you have selected your dog so that you and your loved ones can have a companion, a protector, a friend and a four-legged family member. You invest time, money and effort to care for and train the family's new charge. Of course, this chosen canine behaves perfectly! Well, perfectly like a *dog*.

**THINK LIKE A DOG**
Dogs do not think like humans, nor do humans think like dogs, though we try. Unfortunately, a dog is incapable of compre-hending how humans think, so the responsibility falls on the owner to adopt a proper canine mindset. Dogs cannot rationalise, and dogs exist in the present moment. Many dog owners make the mistake in training of thinking that they can reprimand their dog for something he did a while ago. Basically, you cannot even reprimand a dog for something he did 20 seconds ago! Either catch him in the act or forget it! It is a waste of your and your dog's time—in his mind, you are reprimanding him for whatever he is doing at that moment.

The following behavioural problems represent some which owners most commonly encounter. Every dog is unique and every situation is unique. No author could purport to solve your Deerhound's problems simply by reading a script. Here we outline some basic 'dogspeak' so that owners' chances of solving behavioural problems are increased. Discuss bad habits with your veterinary surgeon and he/she can recommend a behavioural specialist to consult in appropriate cases. Since behavioural abnormalities are the main reason owners abandon their pets, we hope that you will make a valiant effort to solve your Deerhound's problems. Patience and understanding are virtues that must dwell in every pet-loving household.

**SEPARATION ANXIETY**
Recognised by behaviourists as the most common form of stress for dogs, separation anxiety can also lead to destructive behaviours in your dog. It's more than your Deerhound's howling his displeasure at your leaving the

house and his being left alone. This is a normal reaction, no different from the child who cries as his mother leaves him on the first day at school. Separation anxiety is more serious. In fact, if you are constantly with your dog, he will come to expect you with him all of the time, making it even more traumatic for him when you are not there.

Obviously, you enjoy spending time with your dog, and he thrives on your love and attention. However, it should not become a dependent relationship in which he is heartbroken without you. This broken heart can also bring on destructive behaviour as well as loss of appetite, depression and lack of interest in play and interaction. Canine behaviourists have been spending much time and energy to help owners better understand the significance of this stressful condition.

One thing you can do to minimise separation anxiety is to make your entrances and exits as low-key as possible. Do not give your dog a long drawn-out goodbye, and do not overly lavish him with hugs and kisses when you return. This is giving in to the attention that he craves, and it will only make him miss it more when you are away. Another thing you can try is to give your dog a treat when you leave; this will not only keep him occupied and keep

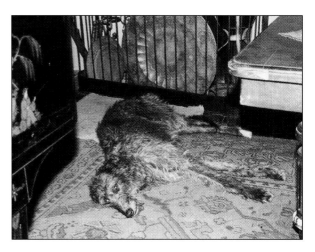

his mind off the fact that you have just left, but it will also help him associate your leaving with a pleasant experience.

You may have to accustom your dog to being left alone at intervals. Of course, when your dog starts whimpering as you approach the door, your first instinct will be to run to him and comfort him, but do not do it!

Separation anxiety can cause a dog to behave like he's suffering from a broken heart.

### I'M HOME!
Dogs left alone for varying lengths of time may often react wildly when their owners return. Sometimes they run, jump, bite, chew, tear things apart, wet themselves, gobble their food or behave in very undisciplined ways. If your dog behaves in this manner upon your return home, allow him to calm down before greeting him or he will consider your attention as a reward for his antics.

Really—eventually he will adjust to your absence. His anxiety stems from being placed in an unfamiliar situation; by familiarising him with being alone, he will learn that he will survive. That is not to say you should purposely leave your dog home alone, but the dog needs to know that, while he can depend on you for his care, you do not have to be by his side 24 hours a day. Some behaviourists recommend tiring the dog out before you leave home—take him for a good long walk or engage in a game of fetch in the garden.

When the dog is alone in the house, he should be placed in his designated area or crate—another distinct advantage to crate training your dog. The crate should be placed in his familiar happy family area, where he normally sleeps and already feels comfortable, thereby making him feel more at ease when he is alone. Be sure to give the dog a special chew toy to enjoy while he settles into his place.

**AGGRESSION**
This is a problem that concerns all responsible dog owners. Aggression can be a very big problem in dogs, and, when not controlled, always becomes dangerous. An aggressive dog, no matter the size, may lunge at, bite or even attack a person or another dog. Generally, Deerhounds are not aggressive, but some males can become bitch-orientated at about two years of age. Any sign of males' showing aggression toward other male dogs must be stopped absolutely immediately and firmly. The dog must be taught a lesson before bad habits form, and must respect the

Aggression can stem from a dog's trying to be the dominant one in your family pack. Dogs learn pack order and etiquette at an early age through play with their littermates.

authority of his owner.

Aggressive behaviour is not to be tolerated. It is more than just inappropriate behaviour; it is painful for a family to watch their dog become unpredictable in his behaviour to the point where they are afraid of him. While not all aggressive behaviour is dangerous, growling, baring teeth, etc., can be frightening. It is important to ascertain why the dog is acting in this manner. Aggression is a display of dominance, and the dog should not have the dominant role in its pack, which is, in this case, your family.

It is important not to challenge an aggressive dog, as this could provoke an attack. Observe your Deerhound's body language. Does he make direct eye contact and stare? Does he try to make himself as large as possible: ears pricked, chest out, tail erect? Height and size signify authority in a dog pack—being taller or 'above' another dog literally means that he is 'above' in social status. These body signals tell you that your Deerhound thinks he is in charge, a problem that needs to be addressed. An aggressive dog is unpredictable; you never know when he is going to strike and what he is going to do. You cannot understand why a dog that is playful one minute is growling the next.

Fear is a common cause of aggression in dogs. Perhaps your

Dogs should always be introduced under supervision and given some time to get acquainted. This Deerhound and Dachshund seem like old friends!

Deerhound had a negative experience as a puppy, which causes him to be fearful when a similar situation presents itself later in life. The dog may act aggressively in order to protect himself from whatever is making him afraid. It is not always easy to determine what is making your dog fearful, but if you can isolate what brings out the fear reaction, you can help the dog get over it. Supervise your Deerhound's interactions with people and other dogs, and praise the dog when it goes well. If he starts to act aggressively in a situation, correct him and remove him from the situation. Do not let people approach the dog and start petting him without your express permission. That way, you can have the dog sit to accept petting, and praise him when he behaves properly. You are focusing on praise and on modifying his behaviour by rewarding him when he acts appropriately. By being gentle and by supervising his interactions, you are showing him that there is no need to be afraid or defensive.

The best solution is to consult a behavioural specialist, one who has experience with the sighthound breeds if possible. Together, perhaps you can pinpoint the cause of your dog's aggression and do something about it. An aggressive dog cannot be trusted, and a dog that cannot be trusted is not safe to have as a family pet. If, very unusually, you find that your Deerhound has become untrustworthy and you feel it necessary to seek a new home with a more suitable family and environment, explain fully to the new owners all your reasons for rehoming the dog to be fair to all concerned. In the very worst case, you will have to consider euthanasia.

### AGGRESSION TOWARD OTHER DOGS

A dog's aggressive behaviour toward another dog stems from not enough exposure to other dogs at an early age. If other dogs make your Deerhound nervous and agitated, he will lash out as a protective mechanism. A dog that has not received sufficient exposure to other canines tends to think that he is the only dog on the planet. The animal becomes so dominant that he does not even show signs that he is fearful or threatened. Without growling or any other physical signal as a warning, he will lunge at and bite the other dog. A way to correct this is to let your Deerhound approach another dog when walking on lead. Watch very closely and, at the first sign of aggression, correct your Deerhound and pull him away. Scold him for any sign of discomfort, and then praise him when he ignores the other dog. Keep this up until either he stops the aggressive behaviour, learns to ignore other dogs or even accepts other dogs. Praise him lavishly for any correct behaviour

### DOMINANT AGGRESSION

A social hierarchy is firmly established in a wild dog pack. The dog wants to dominate those under him and please those above him. Dogs know that there must be a leader. If you are not the obvious choice for emperor, the dog will assume the throne! These conflicting innate desires are what a dog owner is up against when he sets about training a dog. In training a dog to obey commands, the owner is reinforcing that he is the top dog in the 'pack' and that the dog should, and should want to, serve his superior. Thus, the owner is suppressing the dog's urge to dominate by modifying his behaviour and making him obedient.

An important part of training is taking every opportunity to reinforce that you are the leader. The simple action of making your Deerhound sit to wait for his food instead of allowing him to run up to get it when he wants it says that you control when he eats; he is dependent on you for food. Although it may be difficult, do not give in to your dog's wishes every time he whines at you or looks at you with pleading eyes. It is a constant effort to show the dog that his place in the pack is at the bottom. This is not meant to sound cruel or inhumane. You love your Deerhound and you should treat him with care and affection. You (hopefully) did not get a dog just so you could control another creature. Dog training is not about being cruel or feeling important, it is about moulding the dog's behaviour into what is acceptable and teaching him to live by your rules. In theory, it is quite simple: catch him in appropriate behaviour and reward him for it. Add a dog into the equation and it becomes a bit more trying, but as a rule of thumb, positive reinforcement is what works best.

With a dominant dog, punish-

What a big toy...and all for me! You'd be surprised at what your pup finds chewable, especially if bored or not given enough activity.

ment and negative reinforcement can have the opposite effect of what you are after. It can make a dog fearful and/or act out aggressively if he feels he is being challenged. Remember, a dominant dog perceives himself at the top of the social heap and will fight to defend his perceived status. The best way to prevent that is to never give him reason to think that he is in control in the first place. If you are having trouble training your Deerhound and it seems as if he is constantly challenging your authority, seek the help of an obedience trainer or behavioural specialist. A professional will work with both you and your dog to teach you effective techniques to use at home. Beware of trainers who rely on excessively harsh methods; scolding is necessary now and then, but the focus in your training should always be on positive reinforcement.

## SEXUAL BEHAVIOUR

Dogs exhibit certain sexual behaviours that may have influenced your choice of male or female when you first purchased your Deerhound. To a certain extent, spaying/neutering will eliminate these behaviours, but if you are purchasing a dog that you wish to breed from, you should be aware of what you will have to deal with throughout the dog's life.

Female dogs usually have two oestruses per year, with each season lasting about three weeks. These are the only times in which a female dog will mate, and she usually will not allow this until the second week of the cycle, although this varies from bitch to bitch. If not bred during the heat cycle, it is not uncommon for a bitch to experience a false pregnancy, in which her mammary glands swell and she exhibits maternal tendencies toward toys or other objects.

With male dogs, owners must be aware that whole dogs (dogs who are not neutered) have the natural inclination to mark their territory. Males mark their territory by spraying small

amounts of urine as they lift their legs in a macho ritual. Marking can occur both outdoors in the garden and around the neighbourhood as well as indoors on furniture legs, curtains and the sofa. Such behaviour can be very frustrating for the owner; early training is strongly urged before the 'urge' strikes your dog. Neutering the male at an appropriate early age can solve this problem before it becomes a habit.

Other problems associated with males are wandering and mounting. Both of these habits, of course, belong to the unneutered dog, whose sexual drive leads him away from home in search of the bitch in heat. Males will mount females in heat, as well as any other dog, male or female, that happens to catch their fancy. Other possible mounting partners include his owner, the furniture, guests to the home and strangers on the street. Discourage such behaviour early on.

Owners must further recognise that mounting is not merely a sexual expression but also one of dominance. Be consistent and be persistent, and you will find that you can 'move mounters.'

## CHEWING

The national canine pastime is chewing! Every dog loves to sink his 'canines' into a tasty bone, but sometimes that bone is in his owner's hand! Puppies need to chew, to massage their gums, to make their new teeth feel better and to exercise their jaws. This is a natural behaviour that is deeply embedded in all things canine. Our role as owners is not to stop the dog's chewing, but rather to redirect it to positive, chew-worthy objects. Be an informed owner and purchase proper chew toys, like strong nylon bones, that will not splinter. Be sure that the objects are safe and durable, since your dog's safety is at risk. Again, the owner is responsible for ensuring a dog-proof environment.

The best answer is prevention; that is, put your shoes, handbags and other tasty objects in their proper places (out of the reach of the growing canine mouth). Direct puppies to their toys whenever you see them 'tasting' the furniture legs or the leg of your trousers. Make a loud noise to attract the pup's attention and immediately escort him to his chew toy and engage him with the toy for at least four minutes, praising and encouraging him all the while. An array of safe, interesting chew toys will keep your dog's mind and teeth occupied and distracted from chewing on things he shouldn't.

Some trainers recommend deterrents, such as hot pepper, a bitter spice or a product designed for this purpose, to discourage the dog from chewing unwanted objects. Test these products to see which works best before investing in large quantities.

**JUMPING UP**
Jumping up is a dog's friendly way of saying hello! Many a dog owner does not mind when his dog jumps up. The problem arises when guests come to the house and the dog greets them in the same manner—whether they like it or not! However friendly the greeting may be, the chances are that your visitors will not appreciate your dog's enthusiasm...especially with a dog the size of a Deerhound. The dog will not be able to distinguish upon whom he can jump and whom he cannot. Therefore, it is probably best to discourage this behaviour entirely.

Pick a command such as 'Off,' (avoid using 'Down' since you will use that for the dog to lie down) and tell him 'Off' when he jumps up. Place him on the ground on all fours and have him sit, praising him the whole time. Always lavish him with praise and petting when he is in the sit position. In this way, you can give him a warm affectionate greeting, let him know that you are as excited to see him as he is to see you and instil good manners at the same time!

## DIGGING

Digging, which is seen as a destructive behaviour to humans, is actually quite a natural behaviour in dogs. Although terriers (the 'earth dogs') are most associated with digging, any dog's desire to dig can be irrepressible and most frustrating to his owners. When digging occurs in your garden, it is actually a normal behaviour redirected into something the dog can do in his everyday life. In the wild, a dog would be actively seeking food, making his own shelter, etc. He would be using his paws in a purposeful manner for his survival. Since you provide him with food and shelter, he has no need to use his paws for these purposes, and so the energy that he would be using may manifest itself in the form of craters all over your garden and flower beds.

Perhaps your dog is digging as a reaction to boredom—it is somewhat similar to your eating a whole bag of crisps in front of the TV—because they are there and there is nothing better to do! Basically, the answer is to provide the dog with adequate play and exercise so that his mind and paws are occupied, and so that he feels as if he is doing something useful.

Of course, digging is easiest to control if it is stopped as soon as possible, but it is often hard to catch a dog in the act. If your dog is a compulsive digger and is not easily distracted by other activities, you can designate an area on your property where he is allowed to dig. If you catch him digging in an off-limits area of the garden, immediately bring him to the approved area and praise him for digging there. Keep a close eye on him so that you can catch him in the act—that is the only way to make him understand what is permitted and what is not. If you take him to a hole he dug an hour ago and tell him 'No,' he will understand that you are not fond of holes, or dirt or flowers. If you catch him while he is stifle-deep in your tulips, that is when he will get your message.

## BARKING

Deerhounds can be vocal as puppies. As adults, however, they do not bark in the way that the scenthound breeds do, and they are certainly not guard dogs. However, Deerhounds do howl, although rarely for long. Times at

### MORE HARM THAN GOOD

Punishment is rarely necessary for a misbehaving dog. Dogs that habitually behave badly probably had a poor education and do not know what is expected of them. They need training. Negative reinforcement on your part usually does more harm than good.

which they howl particularly are when a bitch is in season, when they are waiting for a walk, or when there is a full moon.

If you have a rare Deerhound who has too much to say about everything he sees, hears, smells and thinks he sees, hears and smells, then this habitual barker must be quietened. Such excessive barking is a problem that should be corrected early on, as soon as it surfaces in the puppy. As your Deerhound grows up, you will be able to tell when his barking is purposeful and when it is for no reason. You will become able to distinguish between your dog's different barks and their meanings. For example, the bark when someone comes to the door will be different from the bark when he is excited to see you. It is similar to a person's tone of voice, except that the dog has to rely totally on tone of voice because he does not have the benefit of using words. An incessant barker will be evident at an early age.

There are some things that encourage a dog to bark. For example, if your dog barks non-stop for a few minutes and you give him a treat to quieten him, he believes that you are rewarding him for barking. He will associate barking with getting a treat and will keep doing it until he is rewarded. On the other hand, if you give him a command such as

'Quiet' and praise him after he has stopped barking for a few seconds, he will get the idea that being 'quiet' is what you want him to do.

## FOOD STEALING

Is your dog devising ways of stealing food from your coffee table or kitchen counter? If so, you must answer the following questions: Is your Deerhound hungry, or is he 'constantly famished' like many dogs seem to be? Face it, some dogs are more food-motivated than others. They are totally obsessed by the smell of food and can only think of their next meal. Food stealing is terrific fun and always yields a great reward—FOOD, glorious food.

Your goal as an owner, therefore, is to be sensible about where food is placed in the home and to reprimand your dog whenever he is caught in the act of stealing.

*Although not known as incessant barkers, Deerhounds do sometimes howl, and some have more to say than others.*

# INDEX

# My Deerhound

PUT YOUR PUPPY'S FIRST PICTURE HERE

Dog's Name _____

Date _____ Photographer _____